# GET MORE OUT OF YOUR MARCO POLO GUIDE

IT'S AS SIMPLE AS THIS

**1** go.marco-polo.com/bal

**2** download and discover

# GO!

WORKS OFFLINE!

D1611924

**SYMBOLS**

INSIDER TIP  Insider Tip

★  Highlight

🔘🔘🔘⚫  Best of ...

🔆  Scenic view

🌍  Responsible travel: fair trade principles and the environment respected

**PRICE CATEGORIES HOTELS**

*Expensive*  over 1,800,000 Rp

*Moderate*  750,000–1,800,000 Rp

*Budget*  under 750,000 Rp

The prices are for a double room with breakfast

**PRICE CATEGORIES RESTAURANTS**

*Expensive*  over 180,000 Rp

*Moderate*  90,000–180,000 Rp

*Budget*  under 90,000 Rp

The prices are for a main course and a non-alcoholic drink

# CONTENTS

---

**MAPS IN THE GUIDEBOOK**
(132 A1) Page numbers
and coordinates refer to
the road atlas
(0) Site/address located
off the map
Coordinates are also given
for places that are not
marked on the road atlas
(U A1) refers to the map of
Kuta inside the back cover

(𝄞 A–B 2–3) Refers to the
removable pull-out map
(𝄞 a–b 2–3) Refers to
additional inset maps on
the pull-out map

**INSIDE FRONT COVER:**
The best highlights

**INSIDE BACK COVER:**
Map of Kuta and general map
of Indonesia

# The best MARCO POLO Insider Tips

## Our top 15 Insider Tips

**INSIDER TIP** **Gourmet meets street food**

At the *Ubud Food Festival*, Indonesia's best chefs experiment with traditional ingredients and create new trends → **p. 117**

**INSIDER TIP** **Cocktails on the rocks**

Enjoy a Margarita and listen to cool music relaxing on the balcony of the *Single Fin*, high above the steep cliffs of Uluwatu → **p. 38**

**INSIDER TIP** **Village idyll in the highlands of Bali**

Enjoy the fresh mountain air, lush nature and a great deal of tranquillity in the *Puri Lumbung Cottages* in the small village of Munduk on Lake Tamblingan → **p. 50**

**INSIDER TIP** **Private villa in the fishing village**

*The Kampung* resort has holiday cottages in traditional Javanese style right on the beach at Amed: relax and watch the colourful outriggers → **p. 36**

**INSIDER TIP** **Jungle and mangroves**

The national park jungle and Bali's best diving region are right on the doorstep of *The Menjangan* lifestyle resort → **p. 55**

**INSIDER TIP** **Wallow in nostalgia**

The *Biku* Teahouse in Seminyak serves traditional colonial style afternoon tea – classically English or with tasty delicacies from all over Asia → **p. 61**

**INSIDER TIP** **Far Eastern wellness temple**

Indulge at Seminyak's *Eastern Garden Martha Tilaar Spa*: traditional massages, and herbal medicine combined with a modern biothermal pool and infra-red sauna → **p. 62**

**INSIDER TIP** **Yoga holiday for complete relaxation**

The small *White Lotus* yoga and meditation centre in Ubud offers a private atmosphere, the murmuring river and view of the rice fields included → **p. 70**

**INSIDER TIP Fairytale beach between the cliffs**

Overnight in *Selong Belanak* (photo left): the cliffs are bathed in bewitching light at dawn and dusk → **p. 78**

**INSIDER TIP Sunset beneath the palms**

Genuine island feeling on the beach of the unspoilt *Exile Resort*: you will have Trawangan's best view of the sunset from here → **p. 97**

**INSIDER TIP Chill out at a coral reef**

Go snorkelling straight from the beach and then enjoy delicious cocktails and fresh seafood in *Ana's Warung* on Gili Meno → **p. 94**

**INSIDER TIP Underwater adventure**

Stay at the *Pearl Beach Resort* on Gili Asahan and explore the spectacular underwater world off the coast of Lombok's little-visited Sekotong Peninsula from there → **p. 83**

**INSIDER TIP Between the volcano and the sea**

Stressed tourists can relax and recharge their batteries surrounded by pristine nature: the *Rinjani Mountain Garden* offers idyllic highland surroundings, a natural swimming pool and panoramic views that stretch from the Rinjani Volcano to the Pacific Ocean → **p. 84**

**INSIDER TIP Through the rice fields on a bicycle**

Authentic village life, verdant rice fields, jungle and plantations full of tropical fruit will accompany you on the novel tours organised by *Mountain Bike Lombok* that are also not too strenuous for average cyclists (photo below) → **p. 112**

**INSIDER TIP Dance and play music like the Balinese**

Professional gamelan and dance courses for children and adults are held in the studio of the *Mekar Bhuana Conservatory* in Denpasar → **p. 115**

# BEST OF ...

**FOR FREE**

● *Free flow at a nightclub*

The *Sky Garden Lounge* in Kuta is famous for its bargain all-you-can-eat buffet, which is available from 5pm until 9pm. All drinks included in the price → p. 47

● *Free art in galleries*

Not interested in museums? You can admire Balinese painting and sculptures on your foray into *Ubud's art galleries* – there is no charge for admission and you will often even be served coffee → p. 67

● *Turtles on the beach*

The WWF-funded *Turtle Conservation and Education Center* on Serangan is open for all and the people working there will be happy to tell you about the rescue of these marine creatures threatened by extinction → p. 60

● *No visit to a temple without a sarong*

Wear your own wrap-around *sarong*, which you can buy inexpensively at the market or in a souvenir shop, when you visit a temple. That way you save the money spent hiring a sash and *sarong* → p. 42

● *Sasak handicraft villages*

In Banyumulek and Sukarara, you will be able to go into the *workshops of the potters and weavers* and watch the craftspeople at work. It is then left up to you to decide if you want to buy something in the shop → p. 89

● *Dance in the museum*

Children from various villages practice their dance every Saturday at 4pm in the inner courtyards of the *Bali Museum* in Denpasar – and you will be able to watch them for free → p. 42

● *Performances at the temple festival*

Gamelan, dance and shadow theatre are part of every temple anniversary. Instead of buying tickets for a tourist show, just ask where the next *Odalan festival* is being held (photo) – tourists are welcome if they behave properly → p. 116

◯◯◯◯●●●● Dots in guidebook refer to 'Best of ...' tips

# ONLY IN BALI/LOMBOK/ GILI ISLANDS
## Unique experiences

● *Giant lizards and dwarf deer*

The dividing line between the Asian and Austronesian primeval continents runs between Bali and Lombok and the flora and fauna of both continents mix here. You can experience the unique animal and plant world in the *Rinjani National Park* (photo) – also possible on easy day tours!
→ p. 85

● *Dance trance*

A rare sight for Europeans – and unforgettable: up to one hundred men moving synchronously, calling out rhythmically and walking over glowing goals in a trance as they do so. The *kecak* performances at sunset on the cliffs of *Pura Uluwatu* are particularly impressive → p. 37

● *Colourful processions*

Women dressed in brightly-coloured clothes balance fruit pyramids on their heads; the men beat heavy gongs: on Bali, you never know when you are going to come across a procession. The most impressive are the parades celebrating the *Galungan Festival* → p. 116

● *Between volcanoes and coral reefs*

Something you can only experience on the Gilis – and best of all, on the small hill on *Gili Trawangan:* the Gunung Rijani rises up in the east at dawn and the Gunung Agung shows just how big it is in the west at sunset. In the hours in between, you can explore the fantastic underwater mountains of the coral islands → p. 96

● *Feast on the beach*

Watch the *fishermen of Jimbaran* in the morning as they bring their colourful outriggers with their catches onto land – the same catches that you could find yourself dining on in one of the many *warungs* close by. Just point at what you would like, and your choice will be grilled for you over glowing coconut shells → pp. 37, 38

● *The battle of the packets of rice*

During *Perang Topat* – which always takes place at the beginning of the rainy season in Pura Lingsar – Hindus and Muslim Sasak pelt each other with rice wrapped in palm leaves. The so-called 'Rice Cake War' is a celebration for everyone, no matter which religion they belong to → pp. 82, 116

ONLY IN

# BEST OF ...

## AND IF IT RAINS?
### Activities to brighten your day

● *Art in Nusa Dua*
Immerse yourselves in the magnificent collection of Southeast Asian and Pacific art in the *Museum Pasifika* in Nusa Dua, presented in modern Balinese architecture → p. 37

● *Balinese wine tasting*
There are also vineyards on the island of the gods – you can try the locally produced tipple at the daily tastings in the *Cellardoor* in Kuta → p. 45

● *Feel like a blockbuster?*
Instead of squinting at the poorly copied pirate DVDs in your hotel room on a rainy day, you can sink back into the chairs of the *Beachwalk XXI Premiere* and watch the latest Hollywood and Bollywood blockbusters – as well as Indonesian films – on the big screen → p. 46

● *Shopping and dining*
The chic shopping centre of *Seminyak Village* not only offers outlets with international bathing and surfer fashions, but also plenty of cafés and beauty salons where you can wait for the rain in the pleasantest way possible → p. 61

● *Exotic arts*
You can learn exactly how the Balinese dance and play gamelan instruments, carve, create batiks and make offerings (photo) in the cultural courses offered by the *ARMA Museum* in Ubud → pp. 66, 70

● *Provincial customs*
Learn how the Sasak marry or how they make daggers in the *Museum Nusa Tenggara Barat*: here you can find out all there is to know about the history, traditions and customs of the islands of Lombok and Sumbawa that form the West Nusa Tenggara Province → p. 80

RAIN

● *Elegant sundowners*

When the sinking sun colours the sea orange-red, the time has arrived to order a cocktail in the chic beach restaurant of the *Mahamaya Boutique Resort* on Gili Meno → **p. 94**

● *Oriental wellness palace*

Treat yourself to a day at the luxurious *Prana Spa* in Seminyak: Ayurveda treatments, Balinese herbal scrubs, reflexology and Turkish steam baths are all on offer → **p. 62**

● *Relax above the ocean*

Luxurious *The Damai* is located away from the tourist spots in the hills behind Lovina. Let your eyes wander over the distant ocean as you float in the pool, and enjoy the fabulous meals served in the luscious tropical gardens of this village resort → **p. 48**

● *Yoga on the beach*

Exhale slowly, and inhale the shimmering colours of the sunset with your Gentle Flow: *The Yoga Place* offers daily sunset classes at Exile Beach on Gili Trawangan → **p. 96**

● *Chill, read, feast*

High above Kuta is the *Ashtari*, a combination of lounge and restaurant: large, comfortable floor cushions, a small corner library and Mediterranean treats encourage you to stay here for several hours → **p. 77**

● *Peace in the rice field*

Let the world pass by in a bamboo pavilion in the middle of a rice field, swim at a waterfall or simply enjoy the view – you can do all of this in *Tetebatu* south of the Rinjani → **p. 82**

● *Meditate in a monastery*

The garden of the *Brahmavihara Arama* (photo) makes its way up the hill over several levels. Prayer halls invite one to meditate and meditation courses are also available → **p. 49**

# INTRODUCTION

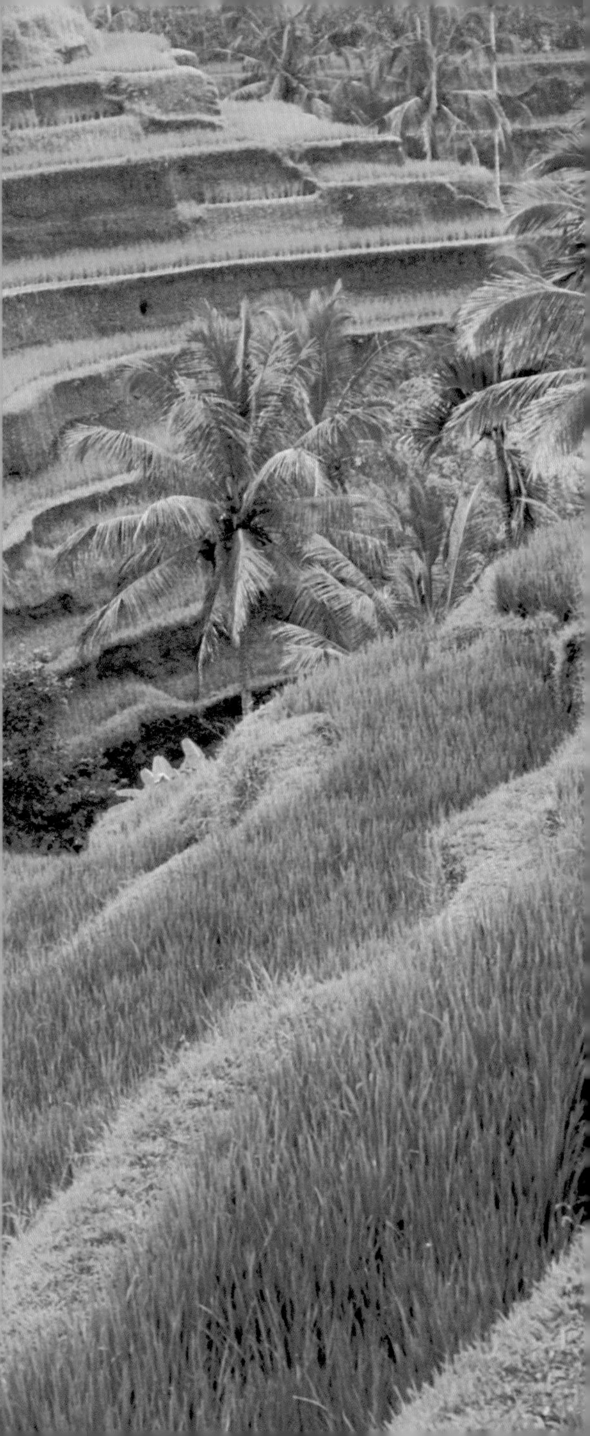

# DISCOVER BALI, LOMBOK AND THE GILI ISLANDS!

Bali, Lombok or the Gilis – the names alone conjure up images of beaches lined with palm trees, coral reefs, of rice terraces and mighty volcanoes. Surfers, divers and mountaineers will find their *paradise* here, while the tourist centres offer all the amenities, from five-star restaurants to oriental spas.

*Bali's* unique culture draws travellers from all around the world: there are very few places where so much natural beauty meets with such a charming lifestyle as here on the 'Island of the Gods'. Surfers find *perfect waves* rolling in beneath the picturesque cliffs and white sandy beaches in the south of the island. A massive mountain range with deep canyons and thundering waterfalls – crowned by the 3148 m/10,328 ft high active volcano, the Gunung Agung, the sacred mountain of the Balinese – towers up in the centre of the island. The verdant green of the rice terraces covers the steep mountain slopes. The more rugged northern section of the island is lined with *beaches of black lava* along the peaceful coast; the offshore reefs are home to a colourful underwater world.

The lush nature, as well as the unique ancient Hindu culture of the island in the Indian Ocean, has fascinated travellers from the West since the 1920s, and yet, in spite of

Photo: Grass harvest on the rice terraces

mass tourism, Bali has retained its own unique charm. As soon as they arrive at the airport, visitors are welcomed with the gentle tones of *gamelan music* and the aroma of clove cigarette smoke. On the ride to the hotel, they can see women by the wayside, dressed in their sarongs, artfully arranging artistically woven small baskets of rice and flowers to protect their homes from demons while motorcycles rattle past.

The first thing the hotel staff do in the morning is to make an offering to the house gods: with their sashes wrapped around them and flowers in their hair, they carry trays of *fruit and incense* to stone altars, junctions and doorways. These offerings and prayers are intended to appease the gods and demons – and thus protect the guests from harm.

## Rituals are part of Balinese daily life

These rituals are not staged for tourists; they are part of everyday life on Bali. The processions on feast days are even more impressive: elegantly dressed Balinese women balance *elaborate towers* of fruit and flowers on their heads accompanied by the booming sounds of gongs. When they take part in the ceremonies in the village temples, the surf instructor with his dreadlocks and the banker from Bali's capital Denpasar both put on the traditional headdress. In some villages, the indigenous Balinese – the Bali Aga – still live according to their old animistic lifestyle.

Bali is not only the last Hindu province in Indonesia – the country with the largest Islamic population in the world – but also the *most cosmopolitan island* in the vast

**From the 1st century**
Indian and Chinese merchants bring Hindu and Buddhist influences

**1478**
The Hindu Majapahit Empire on Java collapses under Islam; the successor to the throne flees to Bali and establishes a new Hindu dynasty

**16th century**
Merchants from Sulawesi bring Islam to Lombok

**1597**
Beginning of Dutch colonisation

**17th century**
Balinese conquer Lombok

One of Bali's most significant temples is the one dedicated to the goddess in Bratan Lake

archipelago. Most Balinese speak at least a little English and tourists are welcome at most ceremonies. There are good reasons for this: tourism, from which more than 80 per cent of the barely 4 million Balinese live, is not least responsible for the fact that the island's Hindu culture has managed to survive so well. *Dances, music and handicrafts* not only fulfil religious purposes but are also a source of income. The government has systematically supported this since the 1960s. That was when hippies took over Bali's beaches with their surfboards and campfires.

The first foreigners to land here were the Dutch. In the middle of the 19th century this turned into a takeover but the Balinese put up fierce resistance: some of the unequal battles ended in the ritual suicide of entire royal courts. The Dutch colonial masters were expelled by the Japanese in the Second World War. In 1949 Bali joined the Republic of Indonesia with Lombok following one year later.

**1846/94**
Start of the Dutch occupation of Bali and Lombok

**1906/08**
*Puputan* (ritual mass suicide) of Balinese royal courts to avoid colonisation

**1942–45**
Japan occupies Indonesia

**17 August 1945**
Indonesia's declaration of independence

**1945–48**
War of Independence against the Dutch

**1955**
First free elections; Sukarno named president

The first Indonesian President Sukarno was faced with the difficult task of forming a single democratic state out of the more than 17,000 islands of the Indonesian archipelago with their different languages, religions and cultures. The attempt ended when the military, under the leadership of General Suharto, took over power in 1965 after it had prevented an alleged coup by the Communist Party. Suharto was forced to resign after protests in 1998. Since then, several heads of government have attempted to promote the *democratisation* process in the largest country in Southeast Asia, which is still plagued by corruption.

> **Bali has become a centre for spas, meditation and yoga**

Due to their special cultural position, the Balinese often feel unaffected by national politics. However, the entire nation was shaken when Islamist suicide attackers exploded bombs in front of nightclubs and tourist restaurants in 2002 and 2005. After the initial shock, the Balinese did all they could to regain the confidence of their guests. Security measures were stepped up and the travel organisations responded with new offers: *ecotourism* for environmentally-conscious travellers, as well as luxurious holidays in secluded villa complexes. In this way, a *new scene*, with Bali as a centre for spas, meditation and yoga, has developed over the last decade. There is also a real boom in the market for organic produce, wellness offers and yoga retreats.

These developments only slowly started to make an impact on the Muslim dominated neighbouring island of *Lombok*. International tourism did not discover the island to the east of Bali until the 1980s and there is only a *good tourist infrastructure* on its western coast. However, following the opening of the new international airport in 2011, the construction boom reached the south coast and there has been a rapid increase in the number of hotels, restaurants and tour operators. Still, the three *Gili Islands* off the northwest coast are still the main attraction: they are a stamping ground for seaside holidaymakers and divers from all around the world. No matter whether it is a family holiday on Gili Air, splendid isolation on Gili Meno or a party trip on Gili Trawangan – everything is possible on the once uninhabited coral islands. Numerous speedboats take tourists directly from Bali to the small car-free islands that are completely surrounded by white sand beaches and also offer a fascinating underwater world. The smaller Gili Islands off the north coast of the Sekotong Peninsula

**1965**
The military prevents an alleged coup; massacre of around 1 million communists

**1966**
General Suharto takes over the government; Bali becomes a tourism destination

**1998**
Following serious unrest, Suharto resigns; economic crisis

**2002 and 2005**
228 people killed in bomb attacks in Kuta and Jimbaran

**2011**
Opening of international airport on Lombok

in the southwest of Lombok are no less appealing, and have an increasing number of lodgings opening their doors.

The majority of the population on Lombok itself still lives off agriculture and fishing, which is precisely what makes the *island so charming*: it is more pristine, more natural and more exciting than its sister island, Bali. This is the right place for those with

The Sasak, Lombok's biggest population group, are Muslim

a sense of adventure. There are very few cultural sites – most date from the period of the Balinese occupation in the 18th and 19th centuries – but the *secluded beaches and fabulous coral reefs* more than make up for this. The breathtaking

**Secluded beaches and coral reefs teeming with life**

Rinjani mountain massif, which covers more than half of the island, towers up in the north. The difficult climb to the summit of the second highest volcano in Indonesia (3726 m/12,224 ft) takes several days but those who persevere will be rewarded with an incomparable panoramic view.

The roads are still bumpy and the hotels few and far between in the dry south and east of the island. This was where *Lombok's indigenous people*, the Sasak, went about their frugal, traditional life. The opening of the international airport only a few miles from Kuta has led to a greater tourism development around the fishing village. In the strict Muslim west, though, backpackers, surfers and divers will continue to relish the solitude of the picturesque bays and white sandy beaches.

# WHAT'S HOT

## ① On the trail

*Trekking* The tours organised by 🟢 *JED (Jl. Kayu Jati 9 y, Seminyak, www.jed.or.id)* provide tourists with genuine insights into Bali's nature and culture. The NGO hires locals who show visitors 'their' island. In this way, traditions and long established structures are protected. Those who follow 🟢 *Pica the trekking guide (from a Swiss NGO, www.zukunft-fuer-kinder.ch/en/)* into the mountain area Muntigunung will not only get an insider's view but will also support disadvantaged Balinese. Many of the tour guides were once beggars.

## Fashionable ②

*Trendy* Fashion Folklore seen differently: More and more national and international fashion designers are transforming traditional made materials into haute couture. *Dwi Iskandar (www.dwi-iskandar.com)* uses batik, songket and tenun fabrics for his creations, while *Bintang Mira (www.bintangmira.com)* uses traditional weaving and printing techniques for her airy dresses. The Italian design duo *Quarzia (Jl. Dewi Sita 7 | Ubud and Jl. Oberoi 3A | Seminyak | www.quarzia.it)* has its elegant batik specially made in Ubud.

## ③ Breathless

*Active* Underwater yoga is a new trend on Bali. Beginners practise in the pool, while those with more experience do it in the ocean. Divers are said to experience a new meditative focus and ability to move their bodies, while the beauty and weightlessness of the underwater world opens up to yogis. Special diving masks are used for controlled breathing through nose and mouth. Courses for all levels are available at the diving school of the *Zen Resort (www.zen harmonydiving.com)* in Seririt and Candidasa.

# Bamboo buildings

*Architecture*  The spectacular bamboo palaces that have been created on Bali by the architectural team of *Ibuku (ibuku.com)*, such as the international *Green School* or private jungle villa *Sharma Springs*, look like something out of a fairy-tale. In the best tradition, incidentally, because Balinese craftsman have been using bamboo, a material with almost unbelievable malleability, to create works of art for ceremonial purposes. Today, villa and restaurant owners all over Bali and the neighbouring islands imitate these airy constructions, although not quite on the same scale as the five-storey luxury *Bamboo Palace (short.travel/bal14)* near Ubud.

# Upcycling

*Shopping*  While waste and tourism don't get on too well, recycling can literally be a nice little earner. Today, more and more recycling companies on Bali collect recyclable waste straight from the consumer and turn it into highly artistic items. 🌀 *Upcycle (Jl. Basangkasa 75)* in Seminyak sells bags and accessories made by village women from former packaging materials, signs or tyres. 🌀 *Lovelife Bali* turns old boxes into cool drinking glasses, chic vases or unusual lamps. They are available to purchase at the *Ego Shop (@SIKA Gallery | Jl. Raya Sanggingan 88x | Ubud)*. 🌀 *The People's Movement (thepeoplesmovement.com)* makes shoes and accessories from plastic bags that are picked up off Bali's beaches.

# IN A NUTSHELL

## BALI-SPIRIT
The sensitive culture and spiritual lifestyle of the Balinese encourages numerous visitors to embark on a voyage of self-discovery. The tourism industry has responded with spa centres, yoga courses and raw food restaurants. Ubud ultimately became a place of pilgrimage for esoterics when the Julia Roberts' film "Eat Pray Love" was shot here. Today, thousands of pilgrims come here for the annual Bali Spirit Festival. The prices are often as lofty as the offers: ecstatic dancing and *Kirtan* song, chakra balancing and sound healing.

## CASTE SYSTEM
The caste system is still important to the Balinese. This is most apparent in the names: on the highest standing are Brahmans (priests) called *Ida Bagus* and *Ida Ayu; Tjokorda* or *Anak Agung* the Ksatria (warriors and nobility). Members of the Wesya caste (merchants) call themselves *Gusti*. 90 per cent of the Balinese belong to the *Sudra* (farmer) caste. They 'number' their children: the first born is named Wayan or Putu, the second child Made or Kadek, the third Nyoman or Komang and the fourth Ketut. They start numbering from the beginning once again after the fifth child. The gender distinction is that men have *I* before their name and women *Ni*.

## COCKFIGHTS
Since 1982, cockfights have only

Life on Bali, Lombok and the Gilis is determined by religions, traditions and the influence of nature

been allowed for so-called 'ritual purposes'. However, this has not prevented the Balinese from holding illegal competitions. The cocks are kept separated from each other in bell-shaped baskets, and their owners take great care of them and their training. Before the fight, sharp blades are tied to the birds' feet.

The bloody spectacle is usually over in just a few seconds. In pre-Hindu times, this ritual was intended to pacify evil demons.

# CREMATION

The Balinese believe that the soul only becomes free after the physical body has been destroyed. Elaborate cremation towers in the form of animals (such as bulls or dragons) are built for the lavish funeral rites. A ritual of this kind is a very expensive affair and many dead are buried for years – and supposedly haunt the cemetery – until the family has saved enough money to be able to afford the expensive ceremony. Poorer families often pool their resources for a mass cremation. The magnificent processions and spectacular cremations are considered major tourist attractions.

by around one hundred men who sit on the ground and then move simultaneously while calling 'cak-ke-cak-ke-cak'. Today's popular *kecak* version was

Despite the Hinduism, a number of animistic rituals are still performed on Bali

# DANCE

On Bali, dances are performed on almost all occasions – at temple festivals, family ceremonies or simply for entertainment. Most of the dances are about characters from the Hindu epics *Ramayana* and *Mahabharata*. The magnificently attired dancers always remain in contact with the ground; each spread of the finger and roll of the eye has a special meaning. Short versions of the most famous dances are performed for tourists: the *barong* describes the battle between a mythical creature and the evil witch Rangda. The graceful *legong* is danced by girls before their first menstruation. The *kecak* is performed

choreographed by the German painter Walter Spies in 1933 for the film "Island of Demons".

# GAMELAN

A gamelan orchestra is made up of at least 30 musicians playing more than 70 instruments – mainly gongs, claves and metallophones, accompanied by flutes and string instruments. There is neither a melody nor are solos performed; the music acts as an accompaniment to dances or shadow theatre performances. The unusual tonality and frequent changes in rhythm can make it difficult for some tourists to get used to when they first hear it.

# HINDUISM

Before the Javanese brought Hinduism to the island, the Balinese practiced animistic spirit worship and believed in a nature pervaded by the divine. Elements of this can still be found in the Balinese Hindu Dharma faith. According to this, the gods live in the mountains and the demons have their home in the sea. Not only in temples, but everywhere on the streets and in their houses, the Balinese make daily offerings to the gods and the demons. The supreme deity for Balinese Hindus is Sanghyang Widhi, in whom the three main gods Brahma, Vishnu and Shiva are embodied. Numerous minor deities and demons live in the rivers, woods and other places.

# ISLAM

Almost 90 per cent of all Indonesians are followers of the Islamic faith. Although only 10 per cent of Bali's population are Muslims, this is as high as 95 per cent on Lombok and the Gilis. Islam has become mixed with local traditions in west and central Lombok. Here, a sip of local palm wine is not considered a sin. However, it is even forbidden to drink beer in the strictly Islamic east of the island. Many Sasak people in the north of Lombok still adhere to *Wetu Telu* ('three elements'), a conglomeration of Islam, animistic and Hindu elements. Wetu Telu followers only pray three times a day and also fast for only three days. However, due to persecution in the past, very few openly profess their faith.

# KITES

When the Balinese fly a kite it – like almost everything else here – has a spiritual significance: it is said that the god Indra liked to play this sport himself. Half of the village is involved in building the kites that can be up to 8 m/26.2 ft long with a tail measuring as much as

another 12 m/39.4 ft. Around 1500 villages compete against each other at the annual Kite Festival in Sanur (July/August). Accompanied by a priest and gamelan music, as many as a dozen men are needed to get the work of art airborne.

# KRETEK

Travellers to Indonesia will be greeted at the airport by the sweetish aroma of *kretek* cigarettes. In 1880, the Javanese Haji Jamahri mixed cloves with tobacco to soothe his asthma: cloves are considered a household remedy for pain relief. This resulted in one of Indonesia's largest industries; 95 per cent of the world's supply of cloves is used in the manufacture of *kretek*.

# KUTA COWBOYS

A suntanned body, long hair and a cheeky grin are their trademarks: the Bali beach boys are always ready, willing and able to be of help to female tourists. Some of them are happy to be a companion for the holiday – often in the hope that it will lead to a lengthier relationship that will bring them financial benefits. The 2010 documentary 'Cowboys in Paradise' gives a detailed description of the background to this indirect form of sexual tourism – much to the annoyance of the Balinese officials. Although most of the beach boys are just harmless show-offs, it is a good idea to be careful.

# PAINTING

Before colonisation, Bali paintings exclusively depicted Hindu myths. A sense of perspective was unknown in the so-called *Wayang* style and colours were only used a fillers. These kinds of pictures are still produced in the village of Kemasan near Klungkung. In the 1920s, the German Walter Spies and Dutchman Rudolf Bonnet, under the patronage of

Prince Cokorda Gede Agung Sukawati, created the Pita Maha school of painting in Ubud. The Europeans introduced modern materials and techniques, but at the same time learnt the traditional art of the Balinese. The Dutchman Arie Smit started the Young Artist school of painting in Penestanan near Ubud in the 1960s. The artists' paintings are characterised by scenes of everyday life in strongly contrasting colours.

# PANCASILA

The Sanskrit word *pancasila* means 'five principles' and has formed the foundation of the Indonesian state since independence. It is represented in the country's coat of arms above the motto 'Unity in Diversity'. The star stands for the belief in a Supreme Being (regardless of religion), the chain for humanity while the banyan tree represents national unity, the buffalo's head democracy and the rice and cotton plants social justice. However, in the past, the varying interpretations of the principle of religion have frequently produced political problems.

# PERMACULTURE

Environmentally friendly agriculture that follows natural cycles and social structures combined with sustainable energy and water supplies: the principles of permaculture were developed in the 1970s by two Australians as a counter concept to industrial agriculture. Bali's first permaculture farms were built back in the 1980s, although organic agriculture did not achieve its breakthrough on the island until the organic boom in the last decade.

# RICE CULTIVATION

Rice is a staple food in Indonesia. However, for the Balinese, it is not simply a plant but a symbol of the goddess of fertility Dewi Sri, who is worshipped in shrines in the fields. The rice fields are irrigated by means of a complex canal system that is strictly controlled by farmer cooperatives *(subak)*. This democratic cultivation system, which is in tune with nature, was recognised by the Unesco as part of the World's Cultural Heritage in 2012. Rice growing is a man's work, but three times a year the whole family helps harvest the crop. On Bali, the picturesque rice terraces cover the fertile volcanic slopes up to an altitude of over 1000 m/3280 ft.

# TEMPLES

Balinese temples are walled compounds; the sky is considered the roof. The entrance is usually a split door guarded by stone demons. The interior of the temple consists of three courtyards with the third – and holiest – facing the mountains. This is where the holy shrines with their multi-tiered roofs are located. Each village has three temples: the *pura puseh* (origin temple) dedicated to Brahma the god of creation. The *pura desa* (village temple) is protected by Vishnu, the preserver, and is the centre of community life. The most rarely visited is the *pura dalem* (temple of the dead) consecrated to Shiva the god of destruction. The most important temple on Bali is the Pura Besakih on the Gunung Agung. It is one of the six most sacred temples, the *sad kahyangan*, that are also known as the 'Great State Temples' or 'Temples of the World', and are built at places of great importance. The other five are the Pura Lempuyang Luhur, Pura Goa Lawah, Pura Luhur Uluwatu, Pura Luhur Batukaru and Pura Pusering Jagat.

# VILLAGE LIFE

Most Balinese live in village communities where everyone has specific obligations to fulfil – but is also given help whenever it is needed. Communal life is regulated by the traditional customary law *(adat)*. The public assembly *(banjar)*, which all married men belong to, decides on all important matters. This community spirit is also reflected in the layout of the village *(desa)*: there is a square *(alun-alun)* with a large banyan tree, which is considered sacred, in the centre with the assembly hall and village temple – and frequently a music pavilion and cockfight arena – grouped around it. The centre of everyday life is the market *(pasar)*. The elected leaders of these traditional village communities also have great influence at the province level.

## WAYANG KULIT

Indonesians had shadow theatres even before Hinduism conquered the islands: it was believed that the shadows could contact the spirits of dead ancestors. A puppeteer *(dalang)* sits in front of a screen with an oil lamp and makes the elaborate figures, embossed on buffalo skin, dance on their bamboo sticks. In catchy singsong, he recounts episodes from the epics *Ramayana* and *Mahabharata*. The gamelan plays in the background. A performance can last all night long; the spectators come and go, eat and chatter away, as they please. Abbreviated versions in English are often available for tourists.

Colourful naive pictures are also created in Bali's artists' studios

# FOOD & DRINK

Spicy coconut curries, delicate meat skewers, crispy chicken and sophisticated fish dishes – the cooking in Bali and Lombok is fiery and full of variety. Rice is always served as an accompaniment – no meal would be complete without it: the Indonesians believe that a person who has not eaten any rice cannot possible be satisfied.

Every morning, the women in the household cook rice and several other dishes for their family. Having a *meal together* is not usual in everyday Indonesian life; everybody eats when they are hungry. This means that, in general, the food is lukewarm or cold – and that is how it is also served in many restaurants. People eat with their fingers or with a spoon and fork. Chopsticks are only used for Chinese dishes such as *mie bakso* (noodle soup with meatballs) or *cap cay* (vegetables sautéed in soy sauce).

However all this changes on feast days: the men take over everything from slaughtering ducks and pigs to grinding the spice pastes when the *ritual dishes* are prepared for Balinese ceremonies. The work often takes days and cooking and eating become a shared social experience.

The *spice pastes* used give each dish its own special flavour. The various ingredients are pounded in a stone trough and usually roasted for a short time. Ginger, turmeric, galangal and coriander are absolutely essential. Lemon grass, limes, salam leaves and tamarind add a touch

Turmeric, coconut, lemon grass – the food on Bali, Lombok and the Gilis is varied and, above all, always fresh

of freshness to the spice mixture and palm sugar and kemiri nuts contribute a certain sweetness. This is all made complete with shrimp paste and chilli. Most restaurants, which are usually open seven days a week, have long since adapted their menus to cater to tourist tastes and serve milder variants of the **Indonesian national dishes** nasi goreng (fried rice), mie goreng (fried noodles), gado-gado (vegetable salad with peanut sauce) and soto ayam (chicken soup with lemon grass and turmeric). These dishes are often accompanied by satay (small skewers of meat) or fried tempe (salty yeast cakes made with soya sprouts), sambal (chilli dip) and krupuk (prawn crackers).

The food served in the kaki lima (mobile food carts) and warungs (street restaurants) is usually more authentic and often much cheaper. In contrast to regular restaurants that usually do not take any orders after 10pm, they can be found open **any time of day or night**. However, you should only eat

# LOCAL SPECIALITIES

**ayam goreng** – crispy fried chicken
**ayam taliwang** – crispy fried or grilled baby chicken with very spicy chilli sauce, from Lombok
**babi guling** – suckling pig filled with spice paste, grilled over an open fire, a Balinese feast dish
**balung nangka** – braised pork ribs with cooked jackfruit
**bebek betutu** – duck stuffed with spice paste and then cooked for hours in banana leaves; Balinese feast dish
**brem** – liquor made from the juice of the Aren palm
**bubuh injin/bubur ketan hitam** – pudding of black sticky rice
**ceramcam** – clear soup with young papaya and fish, chicken or pork
**gado-gado** – vegetable salad with egg and tofu in peanut sauce
**keupat cantok** – rice cooked in small packets of woven palm leaves, with vegetables and peanut sauce
**kue lak-lak** – small round rice flour cakes with palm sugar and grated coconut
**lawar** – minced meat with spice paste, jackfruit, young papaya, green beans and coconut
**lontong** – rice cooked in banana leaves

**mie goreng** – fried noodles, usually served with egg and cucumber (photo left)
**nasi goreng** – fried rice, usually served with egg, krupuk and some salad (photo right)
**nasi kuning** – festive rice, coloured yellow with turmeric and cooked in -coconut milk
**nasi rames** – rice dish with a variety of specialities to sample
**pelecing kangkung** – water spinach with soy sprouts and spicy chilli tomato sauce
**pelecingan** – chicken or fish fried or braised in very hot chilli paste, popular on Lombok
**pepesan ikan** – fish steamed with spices in a banana leaf
**sate ayam/babi/kambing** – small skewers with chicken, pork or goat meat, served with peanut or soy sauce
**sate lilit** – chopped fish or seafood, mixed with coconut and spices and then grilled on small bamboo skewers
**tuak** – wine from the juice of the Aren palm
**urap-urap** – vegetable salad with a dressing of grated coconut, red onions, garlic, salt and chilli

food that has been freshly cooked, fried or grilled. You should avoid food that has been standing uncovered for any length of time – the same applies to water that has not been boiled, ice cubes and sliced fruit (however, you can trust the ice cream and fruit served in the better restaurants). As a rule: if a *warung* is busy then the food is usually good.

After the more recent top restaurants greatly enhanced the traditional cuisine, a large number of *rumah makan* (simple inns) have rediscovered the value of their traditional cuisine and now have a wider selection of local specialities on their menus, but *elaborate festive meals*, such as *babi guling* (suckling pig) and *bebek betutu* (steamed duck), usually have to be ordered in advance.

Desserts are rather uncommon but there is a variety of cakes and puddings made of coconut or sticky rice. *Pisang goreng* (bananas fried in batter) is a popular snack. The *choice of fruit* is absolutely overwhelming: there are sweet mangos and papayas, rambutans, fragrant mangosteens and snake fruit, gigantic jackfruit, tart soursop and – in the eyes of the Indonesians – the queen of all fruits: the spiky durian, whose pungent smell has been known to make the stomach of many tourists churn.

This is served with tea or coffee that is brewed in the cup like mocha. If you don't say something beforehand, you will get it sugary sweet – and, if you order milk, be sure to say you don't mean sticky canned condensed milk *(susu kental)*. However, many cafés have now started making caffè latte and the like, although simple hotels still serve Nescafé at breakfast.

The *fruit juices* are a real highlight: blended with crushed ice and a dash of milk or lime juice, pineapple, melon, guava and avocado become a special treat. Beer is available everywhere and *Storm Beer* (brewed on Bali according to German and English recipes) is especially recommended. Wine lovers will have to dig deeper into their pockets; the most inexpensive are the *Hatten* wines produced on Bali. In contrast to Muslim Lombok, there is a wide range of strong spirits on Bali – from *self-distilled liqueurs* to potent *arak* (rice liquor). But beware:

Exotic fruits are turned into refreshing drinks

stay well away from those self-distilled liqueurs! Adulterated alcohol has already led to several cases of severe methanol poisoning on Bali and Lombok.

If your stomach plays up after all of these unaccustomed foods, it is a good idea to reach for a *kelapa muda* (young coconut): its refreshing water is said to have curative powers.

Online restaurant guides for Bali: *www.balieats.com, balifoodandfun.com, www.bali-indonesia.com/dining*.

# SHOPPING

Bali is a veritable shopper's paradise – clothing, arts and crafts, as well as jewellery are available in every price range. Indonesians come from across the country to the arts and crafts market in Sukawati, which is located 20 km/12.4 mi north of Sanur. This is where useful and decorative items from Bali, Lombok and Java are sold. Lombok in particular is famous for its woven fabrics and ceramics. The most inexpensive places to buy these are where they are made or at the market – but there, you will have to bargain. As a rule of thumb: take off at least 50 per cent of the first price asked by the merchant. If you are planning on making a lot of purchases then get up early: the traders believe that a day's success depends on the first sale and they often offer lower prices in the morning. The shops in the tourist centres usually have fixed prices but they are more expensive. Beware of buying antiques – very few of them are really old.

## CARVINGS

Mythical figures, masks, stylised fruit or complete door frames: the Balinese carve just about everything. The wood carvers in the village of Mas near Ubud are real masters of their art.

## CERAMICS

Pejaten on Bali is famous for its colourful, elaborately decorated ceramics. However, most of the pottery comes from Lombok: the Sasak in Banyumulek and Masbagik produce simple, elegant terracotta goods.

## FABRICS

Almost all of the classic batik fabrics come from Java but the Balinese have adapted the technique and created their own motifs. Good quality is recognisable if the patterns are equally distinct on both sides of the fabric. *Ikat* woven fabrics are typical of Bali and Lombok, they can take weeks or even months to make. With *ikat* you should pay particular attention to the quality of the colours. *Geringsing* fabrics from the Bali Aga village of Tenganan are very special: the fabric is considered sacred and only a few women are still able to produce these extremely rare fabrics. The double-sided patterns are created using the highly complicated double

## Colourful fabrics, shadow puppets, pearl necklaces and wickerwork – the souvenirs on Bali, Lombok and the Gilis are plentiful

*ikat* process and can consequently cost millions of Indonesian rupiah.

## JEWELLERY

There are good silver and goldsmiths on Bali. The most famous village for jewellery is Celuk near Ubud but it is unfortunately overrun by tourist buses. **INSIDER TIP** Beautiful champagne-coloured pearls come from Lombok but there are also glistening black and pink pearls imported from Tahiti and China respectively. The coloured semi-precious stones usually come from Kalimantan. If you are interested in very good quality, you should buy only in recommended shops.

## KRIS

These ornate daggers are said to have spiritual powers and are essential items at traditional dances and ceremonies and are important for the status of a man who inherits his father's weapon. High-quality *kris* are available in good antique shops; cheaper versions can be bought in the silversmiths' village of Celuk near Ubud.

## WAYANG

Beautiful shadow theatre puppets *(wayang kulit)* are expensive; they are notable for the pattern of the pressing in buffalo leather. Only if they show signs of having been used can you be sure that they are actually old. The same applies to the wooden marionettes *(wayang golek)*; most of them come from West Java.

## WICKERWORK

Baskets, boxes, bags and coasters made of bamboo, palm leaves or rattan are perfect gifts to take home; they can be put to many uses and are light weight.

# BALI

**Most visitors are overwhelmed by the many exotic impressions that meet them on arrival in Bali: one moment they are in the midst of the chaotic traffic and then, just a few moments later, in the fragrant world of frangipani blossoms, soothing gamelan music and mystical temple ceremonies that dominate the everyday life of the Balinese.**

Each family – and every hotel – pays tribute several times a day to their house gods with offerings of fruit, rice, flowers and incense. Dressed in sarongs, with sashes and headdresses, the staff and shop owners place their gifts in palm-leaf baskets on the small altars. Even more impressive are the holiday processions, when an entire village makes its way – everybody in their finest clothes

accompanied by the sound of loud gongs – to the temple and the women balancing elaborate pyramids of fruit on their heads.

Bali is an enclave in the country with world's largest Muslim population: 87 per cent of the island's 4 million inhabitants are Hindus. As a result of their late colonisation and early tourist development, the Balinese were able to preserve their culture. Their view of the world is formed by their own mythology in which the sea is peopled by demons and the gods live in the mountains. Their most sacred temple, the Pura Besakih, is located on the slopes of the 3148 m/10,328 ft high Gunung Agung volcano, the highest – and holiest – mountain on Bali. Raging rivers flow

Volcanoes and coral reefs, nightclubs and idyllic beaches, shrines and spas – Bali's many facets will surprise you

through the deep gorges, forests and rice terraces run down to the beaches of white sand in the south and volcanic black in the north. The Balinese spend about a third of their time carrying out their traditional obligations to the gods and the community. In Bali, the administration and sections of jurisdiction are still in the hands of the village communities, the *banjar,* which every married man belongs to. However, many Balinese are finding it increasingly difficult to balance their traditions with mod-

ern life. Globalisation has impacted on the small Indonesian island: the around 3 million international tourists not only bring foreign currency, but also a great number of influences from abroad, with them to the 2200 mi$^2$ island. This can be felt most strongly in Kuta where the majority of the visitors are chiefly interested in sea, surfing and partying. There is a string of restaurants, bars and hotels all the way to chic Seminyak 4 km/2.5 mi to the north. In the 1970s, the tourist resort Nusa Dua was established on the beach-

A tropical underwater paradise awaits divers off the coast of Amed

es on the Bukit Peninsula in the south in an attempt to prevent the masses of holidaymakers overrunning the whole island – today, this is a segregated world of hotel complexes.

Tourists who want to get away from the hustle and bustle to relax, snorkel or dive will find what they are looking for in the north and east of the island in Amed, Lovina and Pemuteran. Ubud, on the other hand, became a Mecca for visitors interested in cultural and religion over the last years. A growing number of companies are geared towards a more elite tourism, with exclusive villas and eco-friendly activities – yoga courses and organic cuisine are de rigueur.

# AMED

(137 E4) (*ⁿ N3*) **Rugged hills and small bays characterise the rough beauty of Bali's eastern coast.**

The stretch of the coast south of the fishing village of Amed was once particularly poor, that has since changed and it has developed into a haven for travellers who want to escape the crowded tourist centres: in the past ten years, hotels and restaurants have multiplied along the narrow coastal road that runs from Amed via *Jemeluk*, *Bunutan*, *Lipah* and *Selang* to the south. In spite of this, Amed has remained peaceful making it possible for families and diving enthusiasts to have a relaxing holiday there. Most of the – usually rather small – holiday places are either located high up on the cliffs or on the dark, sandy beaches that are ideal for bathing or snorkelling. At dusk you can watch the fishermen set out to sea in their outrigger boats. In contrast, there is little in the way of shopping or nightlife in Amed.

You can cross over to the Gilis from Amed *(45 minutes; Kuda Hitam Express | www. kudahitamexpress.com, Gili Sea Express | www.gili-sea-express.com, Freebird Express | freebird-express.com).*

## FOOD & DRINK

### CELAGI

Unpretentious restaurant right on the beach with fresh Balinese and European dishes, seafood and desserts. *Jemeluk | tel. 0859 35 02 66 19 | Budget*

## SAILS ☆
Fresh seafood, steaks and delicious desserts served on an airy terrace high above the sea. *Lean Beach | tel. 0363 2 20 06 | Moderate*

INSIDER TIP ▶ **WAWA WEWE BEACH**
The fourth branch of this family business offers simple but good Western and Indonesian cuisine and is a meeting place for locals and tourists who gather here for cocktails and live music (Mon and Thu). *Amed | tel. 0363 2 35 22 | Budget–Moderate*

### SPORTS & ACTIVITIES

Amed is particularly attractive for divers and snorkellers: you can set out on your underwater safari from most of the bays and be sure to find colourful corals and schools of fish – the best are in Jemeluk and Lipah. The reef off the coast at *Jemeluk* and the small island *Gili Selang* are very popular diving spots. There is a spectacular coral wall, as well as an American supply ship from the Second World War that is covered with coral, somewhat further to the north off the coast at *Tulamben* – this is one of the main attractions for divers in Bali. In recent years, various international resorts with their own diving schools have opened their doors here. The journey from Amed only takes around half an hour, but it is even faster by boat. *Jukung Dive (Amed | tel. 0363 2 34 69 | www.jukungdivebali.com)* and *Eco Dive (Jemeluk | tel. 0363 2 34 82 | www.ecodivebali.com)* offer diving courses and tours and *Amed Bali Tour (tel. 0852 3869 2853 | www.amedbali.tour.com)* organises trips out to sea on fishing boats.

### WHERE TO STAY

**BLUE MOON VILLAS** ☆
Spacious bungalows on the steep slope at Selang; sea view from all the rooms, excellent restaurant, two pools and spa. *34 rooms | Selang | tel. 0363 2 14 28 | www.bluemoonvilla.com | Moderate*

**MARCO POLO HIGHLIGHTS**

# AMED

Once a royal refuge, now a popular leisure area: Ujung Water Palace

**INSIDER TIP** THE KAMPUNG

Two traditional Javanese wooden houses with pool directly on the beach; cleaning and a private dining service. *5 rooms | Jl. Abang-Adem | Bunutan | tel. 0363 23 05 8 | www.thekampung.com | Moderate*

**PALM GARDEN AMED BEACH & SPA RESORT**

Modern bungalow complex with pool, spa and restaurant on the beach, that is built according to feng shui principles. *11 bungalows | Lean Village | Bunutan | tel. 0828 97 69 18 50 | www.palmgarden amed.com | Expensive*

**HOTEL UYAH AMED**

Eco-resort with solar energy that has two pools, a spa and restaurant, and is well integrated into the village. *27 bungalows | Amed | tel. 0363 23 46 2 | www.hoteluyah.com | Budget*

## WHERE TO GO

**AMLAPURA (137 E5) (*M N4*)**

The old seat of the once-powerful Karangasem Kingdom is around 25 km/15.5 mi south of Amed. Today it is a small

district capital with a population of 40,000. However, it is still worth making a stopover to stroll through the narrow streets with their Chinese shops and Muslim *warungs* and visit the two royal palaces: the *Puri Agung (daily 8am–5pm | entrance fee 10,000 Rp)* in Dutch colonial style was a gift from the occupiers and, complete with its water pavilion, is still well preserved. In contrast, the expansive 18th century complex of the *Puri Gede (daily 8am–5pm | entrance fee 10,000 Rp)* is rather dilapidated but there are some interesting pictures and insignias of power waiting to be discovered.

**TIRTAGANGGA (137 D5) (*M N4*)**

The sacred springs of Tirtagangga ('Holy Water of the Ganges'), around which the last King of Karangasem had a park laid out in 1948, are surrounded by rice terraces 18 km/11.2 mi southwest of Amed. Several pools, with ornate waterspouts and statues, splash down over three levels in the luxuriant garden. It is possible to swim in two of the pools if you pay an extra fee *(10,000 Rp)*. *Daily 8am–6pm | entrance fee 20,000 Rp.*

## UJUNG WATER PALACE
### (137 E5) (*N4*)

The *Taman Soekasada Ujung (daily 8am–5pm | entrance fee 35,000 Rp)*, which the King of Karangasem had built as his family residence in 1921, lies 30 km/18.6 mi south of Amed. It was severely damaged by an earthquake in 1979 and the renovations that were carried out are a bit too modern; however, the pools and garden still attract visitors to take a stroll and admire the view of the Gunung Agung. A ☀ winding coastal road leads back to Amed from Ujung. If you decide that you want to enjoy the peaceful atmosphere a little longer, you can spend the night in one of the seven airy villas in the *Seraya Shores Resort (tel. 0812 36 11 93 58 | www.serayashores.com | Moderate)* and enjoy the pool above the ocean and a healthy table d'hôte meal that is made using the fresh ingredients the chef bought that day.

# BUKIT PENINSULA

**(138–139 B–D 5–6) (*H–J 7–8*) The Bukit Badung Peninsula – often simply called 'Bukit' (hill) – hangs like a droplet from the southern tip of Bali.**
Previously, the extremely dry climate meant that the peninsula was hardly inhabited but today the – up to 200 m/656 ft high – limestone cliffs have become famous as the 'millionaire mile'. Many luxurious resorts are opening high up on the spectacular cliffs and Kuta's club scene now also stretches this far. As early as in the 1970s, the government established the hotel city *Nusa Dua* on the eastern beach of the peninsula in an effort to better channel mass tourism. Three heavily guarded gates lead from the small harbour town of *Tanjung Be-*

*noa* into the isolated five-star world that offers tourists everything they want – except genuine Balinese life. A better place to observe that is in ● *Jimbaran* on the west coast where the colourful fishing boats come back in the morning and evening and sell their catch to the row of the simple restaurants along the beach. The area is especially popular with surfers who come to enjoy the bays in the southwest.

### SIGHTSEEING

#### MUSEUM PASIFIKA ●
This spacious museum in modern Balinese architectural style is in the middle of the Nusa Dua hotel complex and not only has art from Indonesia but also from Europe, Indo-China, East Asia and the Pacific islands. *Daily 10am–6pm | entrance fee 70,000 Rp | Block P | Nusa Dua*

#### PURA LUHUR ULUWATU ★ ☀
This 11th century temple, standing 80 m/262.5 ft above the surf, was built to honour the goddess of the sea, Dewi Danu, and is one of the six holiest temples in Bali. A staircase lined with frangipani trees leads to the outer courtyard of the temple whose curved door is guarded by figures of Ganesha.
Scenes from Balinese mythology are carved into the white coral walls. Only Hindus are permitted to enter the middle and inner courtyards. A narrow pathway leads through the temple area along the precipitous coast and has breathtaking views of the sea raging down below. It is especially recommended to visit at sunset when the ● *Kecak* dance is performed in front of the silhouette of the temple. However, be sure that your valuables, cameras and sunglasses are well hidden to protect them from being stolen by the brash monkeys. *Daily 9am–7pm,*

*Kecak daily 6pm | entrance fee 40,000 Rp, Kecak 100,000 Rp.*

## FOOD & DRINK

All of the luxury hotels in Nusa Dua and on the rest of the peninsula have excellent – expensive – restaurants. ● The *warungs* on the beach in Jimbaran are the best places to go for great – inexpensive – seafood.

### BALIQUE RESTAURANT
Delicious fusion cuisine in airy, sophisticated vintage style architecture. *Jl. Uluwatu 89 | Jimbaran | tel. 0361 70 49 45 | Moderate–Expensive*

### BUDDHA SOUL ☻
The lovely organic restaurant and yoga shop offers "soul food", with plenty of vegetarian dishes and raw food. *Jl. Labuansait | Padang-Padang Beach | tel. 0361 8 95 73 38 | Moderate*

### BUMBU BALI
Award-winning master chef Heinz von Holzen serves an exquisite selection of Balinese dishes, and also offers cooking courses. *Jl. Pratama | Tanjung Benoa | tel. 0361 77 22 99 | Moderate*

### INSIDER TIP SINGLE FIN ☻
Cool surfing club with breathtaking views of the cliffs, pizza, tacos, cocktails and lots of music. *Jl. Mamo | Uluwatu | tel. 0361 76 99 71 | Moderate*

## SPORTS & ACTIVITIES

The large hotels offer all kinds of water sports, as well as tennis courts and luxurious spas. The spectacular waves, which attract surfers from all around the world, are the main attraction in the southwest of the peninsula. Courses can be booked from the *Padang Padang Surf Camp (tel. 0819 99 28 35 49 | www.balisurfingcamp.com)*. Golfers will discover one of Asia's finest courses in the *Bali National Golf Club* in Nusa Dua. The ☻ *New Kuta Golf* in Pecatu with sea views *(information under short.travel/bal6)* is a good alternative.

## BEACHES

The peninsula's most expansive beaches are in the *Nusa Dua* hotel complex. Major sections of the beach at *Tanjung Benoa*, as well as in the south of *Jimbaran*, have also been taken over by hotels. The long strip in front of the fish w*arungs* in Jimbaran is more suitable for going for a walk. The very attractive *Dreamland Beach* is almost always crowded, just like the *Pandawa Beach*. Bingin, Balangan and *Padang-Padang* are three bays that are very popular with surfers and where swimming and snorkelling is also possible but they are somewhat more difficult to reach. However, non-surfers and beginners are well advised to just look at the breakers at *Impossibles, Nyang-Nyang, Suluban* and *Uluwatu*.

## WHERE TO STAY

### BALI BULE HOMESTAY
The beautiful family hotel, with pool and restaurant, is only a five-minute drive away from Suluban and Padang-Padang. Ideal for surfers. *10 rooms | Jl. Pantai Padang-Padang | Uluwatu | tel. 0361 76 99 79 | balibulehomestay.com | Budget*

### BALI REEF RESORT
Well maintained bungalow resort with pool, spa and beach restaurant – particularly suitable for families. *28 rooms | Jl. Pratama | Tanjung Benoa | tel. 0361 77 62 91 | www.balireefresort.com | Expensive*

### JIMBARAN PURI BALI

Chic, designer resort set in a spacious tropical garden. Gigantic pool, spa, restaurant and bar directly on the beach; special offers for families and wedding service. *64 cottages | Jl. Uluwatu, Yoga Perkanthi Lane | Jimbaran | tel. 0361 70 16 05 | short. travel/bal7 | Expensive*

**INSIDER TIP** THE TEMPLE LODGE

Spend the night in one of the seven individually decorated suites on the rocks above Bingin and enjoy organic cuisine, a pool and a spa. Daily yoga classes. *Jl. Pantai | Bingin | tel. 0857 39 01 15 72 | www.thetemplelodge.com | Moderate*

### UDAYANA KINGFISHER ECO LODGE

Located on a hill in the middle of the campus of the Udayana University, this hotel offers a well-planned ecological concept with a peaceful and natural environment far away from the beaten tourist track. *15 rooms, 2 villas for longer stays | Kampus Udayana | Jimbaran | tel. 0361 74 71 93 83 | udayanaecolodge.com | Moderate*

# CANDIDASA

**(133 D6) (ꞁꞁ N5) This former fishing village (pop. 20,000) that is often described as the 'old Bali' has managed to retain its original charm although this is not always apparent at first sight.**

During the tourism boom in the 1970s, the coral reefs off the coast were plundered to provide building material – and, a decade later, the surf had completely destroyed the beach. Today, ugly concrete walls protect the main town from further erosion. However, there are bungalows in palm groves and beautiful beaches to the east and west of the centre. Candidasa is an ideal starting point for excursions into Bali's mountainous eastern region.

## FOOD & DRINK

### LEZAT BEACH RESTAURANT

Balinese specialities, served in an airy pavilion beside the sea. Balinese music in the evenings, with legong dancing on Tuesdays, Thursdays and Saturdays.

The surf off the Bukit peninsula is a real challenge for many surfers

*Jl. Raya Candidasa | tel. 0812 3 94 10 75 | Moderate*

**INSIDER TIP** LOAF CANDIDASA
Fabulous selection of cake and bread, excellent coffee for breakfast, fresh salads and pies for lunch. *Jl. Raya Candidasa | tel. 0813 46 29 98 78 | www.ayutamansari.com | Budget*

### VINCENT'S

Homely restaurant and bar with international cooking and a good selection of cocktails and wine; live jazz. *Jl. Raya Candidasa | tel. 0363 41 3 68 | www.vincentsbali.com | Moderate*

## BEACHES

The beach directly to the east of the main road in Candidasa is rather narrow but the sands widen the further one travels westwards. The unspoiled *Pasir Putih* ('White Sand') beach is very popular: a bumpy road starting about 5 km/3.1 mi northeast of Candidasa leads to a sandy beach surrounded by rocks with crystal-clear water. Very crowded after midday.

## WHERE TO STAY

### ALILA MANGGIS

Elegant hotel complex under coconut palms on the lovely beach to the west of Candidasa. Pool, spa, yoga classes and exquisite restaurant. The eco-conscious management has initiated a waste recycling project in the nearby village. *55 rooms | Buitan Manggis | tel. 0363 4 10 11 | www.alilahotels.com/manggis | Expensive*

**INSIDER TIP** SEA BREEZE
This well maintained complex on the beach at Mendira has a restaurant with a relaxed atmosphere, two pools and a spa. *16 rooms | Mendira Beach | tel. 0363 4 21 49 | www.seabreezecandidasa.com | Moderate*

### VILLA ROSSA

Modern villa development north of Candidasa with a pool, spa and diving school. *20 rooms | Jl. Pantai Indah | tel. 0363 4 20 62 | w_maras@yahoo.com | Moderate*

### THE WATERGARDEN

The hotel's 13 bungalows are hidden between lotus ponds in a lush garden on a slope. Two pools, spa and restaurant. *Jl. Raya Candidasa | tel. 0363 4 15 40 | www.watergardenhotel.com | Expensive*

## WHERE TO GO

### GUNUNG AGUNG
(136–137 C–D 3–4) (*M–N 3–4*)
According to Balinese beliefs, the gods live on the summit of the majestic – usually cloud-capped – 'Great Mountain' (3148 m/10,328 ft) around 30 km/18.6 mi from Candidasa. They showed their displeasure in 1963 when the last eruption of the volcano destroyed large areas of eastern Bali. The strenuous climb up to the 700 m/2297 ft wide crater can be made from *Besakih (around 6 hours for experienced mountaineers)* or from *Pura Pasar Agung (around 4 hours)*. A guide is not obligatory but recommendable.

### PURA BESAKIH
(136 C4) (*L–M4*)
Bali's largest and most important temple, the 'Mother Temple', is around 40 km/24.9 mi northwest of Candidasa. At an altitude of around 1000 m/3280 ft on the slopes of the Gunung Agung, it offers stunning views. Its origins date back to the 11th century and today it consists of 22 temples at various heights on the

The morning mist veils the central temple complex of the Pura Besakih

mountain slopes. The symbolic centre is formed by the *Pura Penataran Agung* with a lotus throne dedicated to the god Shiva. It is only worth visiting Pura Besakih with a knowledgeable guide because the long path from the car park to the temple complex has developed into a tourist trap with dozens of intrusive so-called guides and vendors pestering the visitors. *Daily 8am–5pm | entrance fee 35,000 Rp.*

## TENGANAN ★ (137 D5) *(ᗡ N4–5)*

The Bali Aga, the indigenous population of Bali, live a strictly traditional life in a few secluded villages. Tenganan, 3 km/1.9 mi north of Candidasa, is the only Bali Aga village that is open to tourism. The traditional houses go way up the hill to the left and right of the village square. Visitors who make a donation can take a look inside and watch the people living there making basketwork, manuscripts from the leaves of the lontar palm and the famous *Geringsing* fabrics: only a few women still master the art of producing an *ikat* cloth that is woven on both sides. Creating these expensive fabrics, which are said to have magic powers, can take several years. The young men of the village fight each other with pandanus leaves at the annual *Usaba Sambah Festival* in June.

# DENPASAR

(138–139 C–D4) *(ᗡ J6–7)* **Bali's capital city is characterised by modern commercial centres, administration buildings and more than enough traffic. The 800,000 inhabitants come from all parts of the country and the vibrant life reflects Indonesian reality.**

In the southwest Denpasar merges seamlessly into Seminyak, in the southeast the suburbs stretch as far as Sanur. Most tourists just pass through Denpasar, but the former royal city – which was earlier known as *Badung* – has many beautiful buildings and parks, a historical museum and culture centre. The old royal palace was almost completely destroyed at the time of the Dutch conquest in 1906 and today only the small palaces

# DENPASAR

*Puri Satria (Jl. Veteran), Puri Pemecutan (Jl. Thamrin)* and *Puri Jero Kuta (Jl. Dr. Sutomo)* can be seen. Although the colonial rulers established the seat of their administration in Singaraja, Denpasar had already become an important trading centre in the 1930s – however, it did not achieve its status as Bali's capital city until the year 1958.

## SIGHTSEEING

**ARTS CENTRE TAMAN WEDHI BUDAYA**
The cultural centre is located in a park in the eastern section of Denpasar. The spacious complex includes the art academy, a gallery and three open-air stages. It gets really crowded during the *Bali Arts*

**Jl. Gajah Mada:** Denpasar's main thoroughfare starts south of the bus terminus in the west, where all the intercity buses arrive, and cuts straight through the centre. This is also the site of the two markets, the Pasar Badung and Pasar Kumbasari. If you follow the street about 500 m/1640 ft to the west you reach Puputan Square with the Pura Jagatnatha and the Bali Museum.

*Festival (www.baliartsfestival.com)* that is held every year in June/July. *Mon–Thu, Sat 8am–2.30pm, Fri 8am–12.30pm, during the festival daily 10am–10pm | Jl. Nusa Indah*

**BALI MUSEUM (MUSEUM NEGERI PROPINSI BALI)**
The Bali Provincial Public Museum exhibits prehistoric artefacts, dance costumes, religious objects and gamelan instruments. Today, the museum, which was founded by the Dutch in 1910, is made up of four buildings in Balinese palace and temple architecture from various epochs including the period of the Gelgel and Karangasem dynasties. ● Children's dance groups train in the inner courtyard every Saturday at 4pm *(free admission). Sat–Thu 8am–4pm, Fri 8.30am–12.30pm | entrance fee 20,000 Rp | Jl. Mayor Wisnu*

**PUPUTAN SQUARE**
A memorial on the green square in the centre of Denpasar commemorates the ritual suicides *(puputan)* of the Princes of Badung and Tabanan, who defied the Dutch – unarmed – together with their entire courts in 1906 in order to evade colonisation. Those who were

## LOW BUDGET

Most of the dance and music performances at the *Bali Arts Festival* (June/July) in Denpasar are free and there is much more variety than in the normal shows for tourists.

At the *Ubud Food Festival* (see p. 117) there are various events at which you can sample fresh specialities free of charge.

● Instead of paying the fee to use a *sarong* and sash when you visit the temples in Bali, buy your own inexpensive wrap-around at the start of your holiday and always have it with you.

If you make several trips with the shuttle buses of *Perama Tours (www.peramatour.com)*, you will be given a discount upon presentation of the old tickets.

not slaughtered in the volleys of gunfire killed themselves after the massacre. Today, the square is a popular after work meeting place.

### PURA JAGATNATHA
Located on the eastern side of Puputan Square is Bali's state temple. It was built in 1953 and is dedicated to the supreme

house. It serves coffee roasted in-house, including Kopi Luwak, the world's most expensive variety. *Jl. Gajah Mada 80 | www.kopibali.com*

### PASAR MALAM KERENENG
The lively night market has stalls offering dishes from all over Indonesia. *Jl. Kamboja | Budget*

Masked dancers are among the performers at the Bali Art Festival in Denpasar

deity Sanghyang Widhi who unites Shiva, Brahma and Vishnu in one entity and in this way satisfies the Indonesian national philosophy of *pancasila* (monotheism). The shrine is made of white coral. There are *wayang* performances on full moon nights when the Balinese philosophise, drink and flirt in front of the temple.

## FOOD & DRINK

INSIDER TIP BHINEKA JAYA CAFE
The café run by Bali's best-known coffee producer is actually a colonial era ware-

## SHOPPING

Along with modern shopping malls, Denpasar has several interesting markets: the largest is the *Pasar Badung (Jl. Gajah Mada)* where fresh food can already be bought from 5 o'clock in the morning. The *Pasar Kumbasari* on the other side of the river is the place to go for arts and crafts and souvenirs. The bird market, *Pasar Burung (Jl. Veteran)*, is very colourful but not for the faint of heart; not only feathered creatures, but also other small animals and insects are sold there.

A stroll along Pasar Badung isn't just a treat for (amateur) chefs

## WHERE TO STAY

**INNA BALI**
Denpasar's oldest international hotel, which was built by the Dutch in 1927, still exudes a colonial atmosphere. Restaurant and swimming pool. *71 rooms | Jl. Veteranhotel 3 | tel. 0361 22 56 81 | www. innabali.com | Budget–Moderate*

## INFORMATION

**DENPASAR GOVERNMENT TOURISM OFFICE**
*Jl. Surapati 7 | tel. 0361 23 45 69 | www. balidenpasartourism.com*

# KUTA/LEGIAN

⬛ **MAP INSIDE BACK COVER**
(138 C4–5) (*M H–J7*) **Before the hippies and surfers discovered the mile long beach (with endless rolling waves) in the 1960s, Kuta was a simple fishing village with unpaved roads.**
The only traces of the old village left in what has become Bali's most important

tourist centre (pop. 100,000) are the narrow streets around Poppies Lane. There is an unending press of cars, mopeds and hawkers along the seaside promenade and *Jalan Legian* that links Kuta and Legian. Countless hotels, restaurants and shops are lined up next to each other and the borders to the neighbouring towns of Tuban in the south and Seminyak in the north have ceased to exist: Kuta and Legian have amalgamated to become an urban conglomerate that has now reached the limits of its growth. But it is precisely this pulsating density that is so attractive to surfers and party fans who want to enjoy the sea, sun and the surf during the day and the nightlife after dark. In contrast, somewhat more peaceful Tuban offers everything visitors need for a family holiday from an amusement park to shopping mall.
A memorial at the site of one of the nightclubs commemorates the victims of the bombings in 2002 and 2005 when more than 200 people lost their lives. To this day, the security measures in large hotels and malls are therefore often very strict.

## FOOD & DRINK

### BENE LANE CAFE (U B4) (*b4*)
Popular sports café, serves burgers, steaks and drinks to go with live performances. *Jl. Lebak Bene, Shop 1 | Legian Kelod | tel. 0361 75 98 94 | Budget*

### ENVY (U A5) (*a5*)
The friendly staff in this hip beach lounge serve delicious pasta, steaks, seafood and cocktails. *Jl. Wana Segara 33 | Tuban | tel. 0361 75 25 27 | Moderate–Expensive*

### GABAH RESTAURANT & BAR (U B5) (*b5*)
Restaurant in a central location with dishes from all over Indonesia. *Jl. Bakung Sari | Tuban | tel. 0361 75 18 64 | www.ramayanahotel.com | Expensive*

### KORI RESTAURANT & BAR (U B4) (*b4*)
A peaceful oasis in the heart of Kuta: enjoy the Balinese specialities and international cuisine in a beautiful garden. Cigar and cognac lounge. *Poppies Lane II | Kuta | tel. 0361 75 86 05 | Moderate*

### KUALI RESTAURANT (U B3) (*b3*)
This beach restaurant under giant trees serves generous helpings of Indonesian and Western dishes. *Jl. Arjuna 99 | Legian Kaja | tel. 0361 73 02 45 | Budget–Moderate*

### MADE'S WARUNG I AND II
Always full, the cheerful staff pamper the guests with tasty Indonesian food. *Jl. Pantai Kuta* (U B5) (*b5*) *| tel. 0361 73 21 30 | Kuta and Jl. Raya Seminyak* (U B3) (*b3*) *| Legian | tel. 0361 75 52 97 | Moderate*

### INSIDER TIP PEARL RESTAURANT BALI (U B3) (*b3*)
This elegant restaurant with its exquisite French cuisine is like an oasis in the midst of all the hustle and bustle. Book! *Jl. Arjuna | Legian Kaja | tel. 0819 34 33 40 60 | Expensive*

## SHOPPING

### ASIA LINE HANDICRAFT (U B3) (*b3*)
Indonesian craftsmanship ranging from wooden masks and rattan bags to silver vases of export quality. *Jl. Legian Kaja 457a | Legian Kaja*

### BALI BEACH WALK (U B4) (*b4*)
Smart shopping centre on the beach promenade with native and international food and design outlets. *Jl. Pantai Kuta | Kuta | beachfashionwalkbali.com*

### BIN HOUSE
The wearable Indonesian fashions are handmade using exquisite fabrics and traditional styles. *Discovery Shopping Mall MG 30 | Jl. Kartika Plaza* (U B5) (*b5*) *| Kuta and Made's Warung | Jl. Raya Seminyak* (U B3) (*b3*) *| Seminyak | www.binhouse.com*

### CELLARDOOR ● (U 0) (*0*)
Bali's Hatten Wines shop not only sells their own wines but also those produced by the Dewi Sri distillery and there are daily wine tastings. *Bypass Ngurah Rai 393 | tel. 0361 4 72 13 77 | www.hattenwines.com*

### POKITO 1 (U B4) (*b4*)
The top address for creative fashion for children, with modern batik motifs for little ones up to ten years of age. *Jl. Legian 384 | Kuta | www.facebook.com/pokito.bali*

### RIP CURL LEGIAN MEMORIAL (U B4) (*b4*)
Everything a surfer could design in bamboo architecture. *Jl. Legian 62 | Kuta*

## SPORTS & ACTIVITIES

There are good surfing spots and places to hire equipment everywhere at the beach and you can take courses at the *Pro Surf School (Jl. Pantai Kuta* (U B4) *(ᗰ b4) | Kuta | tel. 0361 75 12 00 | www. prosurfschool.com)*. Those who want to go snorkelling or diving will have to drive a little further because the coast directly

## ENTERTAINMENT

Kuta is the main nightlife area of Bali with countless clubs; the largest are on the *southern section of Jl. Legian*. The entertainment area around Jl. Arjuna, which used to be internationally famous, now moved more to Seminyak. There are more and more new clubs opening on the Bukit Peninsula, too.

Surfers need not wait long for the perfect wave on Kuta's beaches

off Kuta is not suited for those activities. Tours and courses are organised by numerous firms including *Paradise Diving Indonesia (Jl. Arjuna 6a* (U A3) *(ᗰ a3) | Legian | tel. 0811 39 35 15 | www.b-a-l-i. com/english.htm)*.

There are beach massages and spas on every corner. The *DaLa Spa* in the *Villa de Daun Resort (Jl. Legian 123* (U B4) *(ᗰ b4) | Kuta | tel. 0361 75 62 76)*, is considered to be one of Kuta's best but the treatments in *Cozy (Jl. Sunset Blok A3* (U B3) *(ᗰ b3) | Legian | tel. 0361 76 67 62)* are not quite as expensive. The *Waterbom Park (daily 9am–6pm | entrance fee 39 US$ | Jl. Kartika Plaza* (U B5) *(ᗰ b5) | Tuban | www.waterbom-bali.com)* guarantees fun for the whole family.

### BEACHWALK XXI PREMIERE ● (U B4) *(ᗰ b4)*

Luxurious cinema, that mainly shows blockbusters from Hollywood and Asia. *Beachwalk Lantai 2, Jl. Pantai Kuta | Kuta | www.21cineplex.com/theaters*

### BOSHE VVIPCLUB (U 0) *(ᗰ 0)*

A mainly young audience gathers here for the sounds by local DJs and karaoke parties. *Daily 1pm–3am | Bypass Ngurah Rai 89x*

### VILLA COCO (U B3) *(ᗰ b3)*

The beach is ten minutes away from this secluded garden complex, with luxurious private villas, in the heart of Legian. Pool and in-house catering.

19 villas | Jl. Arjuna, Gang Villa Coco | Legian | tel. 0361 73 07 36 | www.villacoco. com | *Expensive*

### OCEAN'S 27 ☀ (U B5) (*□ b5*)
When the sun goes down this beach bar turns into a hip nightclub with international DJs. *Daily 10am–1am | Discovery Esplanade | Jl. Kartika Plaza | Tuban*

### SKY GARDEN LOUNGE ☀ (U B4) (*□ b4*)
Celebrate with a spectacular view over the rooftops of Kuta: a mixed crowd spread over several dance floors and bars. ● All-you-can-eat buffet, drinks included. *Daily 7pm–4am | Jl. Legian 61 | Kuta*

## WHERE TO STAY

### ALAYA RESORT (U B5) (*□ b5*)
Modern designer hotel with every imaginable comfort, restaurant, pool, gym and a branch of the well-known DaLa Spa. *116 rooms | Jl. Kartika Plaza, Gang Puspa Ayu 99 | Tuban | tel. 0361 75 53 80 | www.alayahotels | Expensive*

### DEKUTA BOUTIQUE HOTEL (U B4) (*□ b4*)
Modern hotel catering to families, just steps away from the beach at Legian; with pool and two restaurants. *53 rooms| Jl. Pantai Kuta, Poppies Lane II | tel. 0361 75 38 80 | dekuta.com | Moderate*

### KUTA ECOSTAY ⊕ (U B5) (*□ b5*)
Ecological homestay down a narrow little street that values waste separation and natural wastewater disposal. *16 clean rooms Jl. Pantai Kuta, Gang Lotring 12 | Kuta | tel. 0813 38 67 01 33 | Budget*

### PADMA RESORT (U B3) (*□ b3*)
Large five-star beach hotel in modern Bali style with a variety of restaurants and bars, pool area and spa, sport and children's activities. *409 rooms | Jl. Padma 1 | Legian |*

*tel. 0361 75 21 11 | www.padmaresortlegian. com | Expensive*

### POPPIES COTTAGES I (U B4) (*□ b4*)
A classic in Kuta: a narrow lane with small bungalows set in a tropical garden with pool; five minutes from the beach. *25 bungalows | Poppies Lane I | Kuta | tel. 0361 75 10 59 | www.poppiesbali.com | Moderate*

### PURI DAMAI (U A3) (*□ a3*)
Hotel and pool in a quiet locations, all twelve apartments with their own kitchen and sitting area. Just a five-minute walk to the beach. *Jl. Werkudura | Legian Kaja | tel. 0361 73 06 65 | www.madeswarung.com | Moderate*

### INSIDER TIP TANAYA BED & BREAKFAST (U B3) (*□ b3*)
Reasonably-priced accommodation for budget travellers, with modern, clean rooms. Centrally located. *7 rooms | Jl. Legian 131 | Kuta | tel. 0361 75 62 76 | www. tanaya.com | Budget*

## INFORMATION

### INDONESIA TOURIST INFORMATION (U B4) (*□ b4*)
*Jl. Raya Kuta 2 | Kuta | tel. 0361 76 61 81*

# LOVINA

*(134 C2) (□ G1–2)* **Named after the English word 'love' by the last King of Buleleng, this 10 km/6.2 mi coastline stretches to the west of Singaraja and includes the villages of Anturan, Kalibukbuk and Kaliasem.**
Inspired by the hippies and their peaceful invasion of Bali's north in the 1970s, the Prince realised his ideas of tourism here. Lovina lies on volcanic black sand beaches

and the calm sea is ideal for swimming and snorkelling. Dolphin watching is the main attraction here. Every morning before sunrise, dozens of small outrigger boats set out for the reefs to show tourists the dolphins that can usually be found frolicking there. Lovina has seen better days and this has led to many of the hotels and sections of the beach becoming neglected and besieged by so-called guides looking for work. On the other hand, numerous resorts offering wellness, yoga and meditation holidays are being established at the foot of the nearby mountains. Lovina is an ideal starting point for excursions into the central highlands of Bali.

## FOOD & DRINK

### AKAR CAFE 🌿
Small, fine and eco in every aspect: tasty vegetarian dishes, organic products, agency for yoga courses and even the décor is mint-green. *Jl. Binaria | Kalibukbuk | tel. 0819 15 62 55 25 | Budget–Moderate*

### INSIDER TIP ▶ BAKERY LOVINA
This is the place for a healthy breakfast with muesli, whole-wheat bread, sausages and cheese, as well as a good wine selection and the best pizza in the north of Bali. *Jl. Raya Lovina | Kalibukbuk | tel. 0362 4 22 25 | Moderate*

### MR. DOLPHIN
Popular, simple beach restaurant with good seafood and live music. *Jl. Laviana | Banyualit | tel. 0813 53 27 69 85 | Budget*

## SPORTS & ACTIVITIES

You can get diving and snorkelling equipment from your hotel or from *Spicedive (tel. 0851 00 01 26 66 | short.travel/bal8)*, where you can also book tours and courses. Dolphin tours are offered everywhere

on the beach and can also be organised by your accommodation. You will be able to learn massage techniques yourself in the *Araminth Spa (Jl. Damai | Bhuanasari | tel. 0362 3 43 57 59 | araminthspavillas.com)*. The *Nibbana Bali Resort (Umeanyar | Seririt | tel. 0811 39 77 84)* and the *Zen Resort Bali (Seririt | tel. 0362 9 35 78 | www.zenresortbali. com)* offer wellness and yoga holidays.

## WHERE TO STAY

### THE DAMAI ● 🌙 🌿
Exquisite boutique hotel with 14 stylish bungalows, beautiful pool and spa. Near the mountains but with a view over the sea. Award-winning restaurant serving organic cuisine. *Jl. Damai | Kayuputih | tel. 0362 4 10 08 | www.thedamai.com | Expensive*

### FRANGIPANI BEACH HOTEL
Chic boutique hotel right on the beach, with a view of the rice field. Pool and restaurant. *9 rooms | Jl. Kartika | Kalibukbuk | tel. 0812 3 82 47 79 | www.frangipani beachhotelbali.com | Moderate*

### INSIDER TIP ▶ THE HAMSA RESORT 🌙 🌿
The 13 villas around a pool in a gigantic garden lie high up the mountain above the Singsing Waterfall with a view down to the sea. The services offered include an organic restaurant and Ayurvedic spa, yoga and detoxification treatments. *Jl. Air Terjun Sing Sing | Desa Cempaga | tel. 0813 37 19 49 75 | www.thehamsaresort. com | Moderate*

### HOTEL MELAMUN
Simple, decent hotel with very good service, a beautiful swimming pool and spa; three minutes from the beach. *10 rooms | Jl. Laviana 7 | Banyualit | tel. 0362 4 15 61 | www.melamunhotel.com | Budget*

## WHERE TO GO

### BANJAR (134 B3) (*Ⓜ F2*)

Famous for its hot springs *(Air Panas | daily 8am–6pm | entrance fee 5000 Rp)*, the village of Banjar is only 10 km/6.2 mi to the west of Lovinia. A short footpath leads to three pools with stone waterspouts. It is said that a dip in the 37°C/98.5°F sulphurous water has a curative effect. Bali's only Buddhist monastery the ● ⋙ *Brahmavihara Arama (daily 9am–6pm | entrance for a donation | brahmaviharaarama.com)* lies south of Banjar. A garden with prayer halls climbs up the slope in several tiers: you can meditate there or simply enjoy the view down to the sea from high up. The monastery offers mediation stays lasting several days.

### DANAU BRATAN ⋙ (135 E3–4) (*Ⓜ H–J3*)

The *Bratan Lake* stretches along the road from Singaraja to Bedugul around 20 km/12.4 mi southeast of Lovina. Its main attraction is the fairytale 17th century *Pura Ulun Danu Bratan (daily 7am–7pm | entrance fee 30,000 Rp)*, one of the most important temples and a very popular photo opportunity. The eleven-tiered shrine, dedicated to the goddess of the lake, is located on a small island behind a beautiful garden. The Balinese take part in numerous ceremonies here to pray for sufficient water for their fields.

There are various accommodations and amusement parks near the lake: you can admire the 380 acres of *Botanical Gardens (daily 7am–6pm | entrance fee 7000 Rp, cars 12,000 Rp | Kebun Raya Eka Karya)* in *Candikuning* and also visit the *Bali Treetop Adventure Park (daily 8.30am–6pm | entrance fee 21 US$)*. There is an 18-hole golf course, hotel and spa at the *Bali Handara Kosaido Country Club (www.balihandara kosaido.com)* north of the lake.

### DANAU BUYAN AND TAMBLINGAN ★ ⋙ (135 D3) (*Ⓜ H2*)

The area around the Buyan and Tamblingan lakes, which once formed a single large crater lake, forms the fertile heart of Bali. A road passes coffee plantations on the high bank at the northern

Treatments Indonesian style: bathing in the hot sulphur springs of Banjar

edge. You can walk to the village of *Munduk* (25 km/15.5 mi south of Lovina) on the southern shore, it is scenically located between mountain forests, orchards, and rice and tobacco fields. There is a 2 km/1.2 mi path to a waterfall east of Munduk. If you stay at the ☀ ◉ INSIDERTIP *Puri Lumbung Cottages (tel. 0361 43 70 71 | www.puriumbung. com | Moderate)*, an award-winning eco-resort with 23 cottages converted from old rice granaries with a view as far

## SINGARAJA (135 D1) (*H1*)

With its population of 120,000, the old capital 10 km/6.2 mi east of Lovina is the second largest town on the island. From here the Dutch established their control of Bali and the old harbour and many colonial buildings still bear witness to this period. Muslim and Chinese merchants had already settled here long before that and they still set the tone of life on the streets. The old palace, the *Puri Agung (daily 4am–6pm | entrance for a donation | Jl.*

An idyll that can only be reached via narrow paths: Lake Tamblingan

as the ocean, you will be able to relish the environment for even longer.

### GITGIT WATERFALL
(135 D2) (*H2*)

About 17 km/10.6 mi southeast of Lovina is Bali's highest waterfall which plummets around 40 m/131.3 ft into the depths. A concrete path leads in about 10 minutes from the road to Bedugul past all kinds of kiosks and fruit trees to the natural pool *(daily 8am–5pm | entrance fee 10,000 Rp).*

*Mayor Metra 12 | tel. 0362 2 29 74),* of the Kings of Buleleng was reconstructed at the beginning of the 20th century and today mainly exhibits pictures of the royal family whose descendants still live here. The *Museum Buleleng (Mon–Thu 7am–3pm, Fri 7am–11 am | entrance fee 10,000 Rp | Jl. Veteran 23)* around 200 m/656 ft to the north provides information on the history of the region and life of the last king. Opposite, you can visit the library founded by the Dutch in 1928, the *Gedong Kirtya (Mon–Thu 7am–*

2.30pm, Fri 7am–noon | entrance fee 20,000 Rp | Jl. Veteran 20), where more than 3000 old documents – including ornate lontar-leaf manuscripts and colonial writings – are preserved. There are several impressive temples a few miles to the east of Singaraja. The erotic scenes and caricatures, which also include modern elements such as cars, in the *Pura Dalem* in *Sangsit* and *Jagaraga* show the more frivolous style of the north.

# NUSA LEMBONGAN

(137 D1) (*L–M 6–7*) ⭐ **Tourists who want to escape from all the hustle and bustle in the south of Bali will find what they are looking for here: the pace of life on the little island (4.5 × 2.5 km/ 2.8 × 1.6 mi) 12 km/7.5 mi to the east off the coast of Sanur, is much slower and – with the exception of a few small vans – there are no cars.**

Although there has been an increase in the number of resorts in the last ten years, many of the island's around 5000 inhabitants continue to live from seaweed cultivation. The main village of *Jungutbatu* has a small clinic, receiving post office and a cash machine – which is often out of order. In the village of Lembongan, you can visit an *underground house (daily | admission 20,000 Rp)*. There are seven small temples in all, scattered over the island.

A long reef in the northwest has made Nusa Lembongan a popular destination for surfers. Snorkellers and divers can explore beautiful banks of coral around the neighbouring islands of *Nusa Ceningan* and *Nusa Penida*. The northeast is the region for trips through the mangroves while the secluded bays in the south will make you feel like a modern-day Robinson Crusoe. Almost all of the accommodation is located on the western side of the island – many with spectacular views of the Gunung Agung.

The fastest way from Sanur to Nusa Lembongan is by public ferry *(daily 10.30am, 90 minutes| 100,000 Rp, Perama | daily 10.30am, 90 minutes | 140,000 Rp | www.peramatour.com)* or by speedboat *(30 minutes from 175,000 Rp | Public Boat and private providers | lembonganfastboats. com)*. There are also speedboat connections from Padang Bai and the Gilis *(gili-fastboat.com)*.

## FOOD & DRINK

Most of the accommodations also run small cafés and there are simple *warungs* in the village. The hotel resorts in the southwest offer more elegant dining.

### THE BEACH CLUB AT SANDY BAY
The small bay in the southeast of the island is the perfect place to chill out in the afternoon with a drink by the pool or to have a romantic dinner at night (collection service). *Sandy Bay | tel. 0828 97 00 56 56 | www.sandybaylembongan.com |* *Expensive*

### BLUE CORNER BAR 🌿 ♨
The beach bar is part of the Blue Corner diving centre and eco resort and was built using natural materials. Its comfortable blue beanbags are ideal for tapas and magaritas. Instead of concrete walls, plants protect this stretch of the coastline from surf erosion. Waste recycling. *Blue Corner Beach | north of Jungutbatu | tel. 0819 16 23 10 54 | Budget*

## SPORTS & ACTIVITIES

There are three popular spots for surfing right in front of *Jungutbatu* – they are

# NUSA LEMBONGAN

popular with people on the beach too as there is always plenty to see. All of the accommodation options organise swimming and snorkelling trips to the more remote beaches. The possibilities for diving and snorkelling around *Nusa Ceningan* and *Nusa Penida* are excel-

*Coconut Beach* at the southern end of the main beach leads over the rocks to *Mushroom Bay,* which is also accessible by boat. From the village of Lembongan some bumpy roads lead to *Tamarind Bay, Sandy Bay* and the wild and romantic *Dream Beach*.

The view of Nusa Lembongan is particularly lovely at sundown

lent. Courses can be booked from *World Diving (Pondok Baruna | Jungutbatu | tel. 0812 3 90 06 86 | www.world-diving. com)* and ⊙ *Big Fish (Secret Garden | Jungutbatu | tel. 0813 53 13 68 61 | www. bigfishdiving.com),* an organisation that supports initiatives to preserve the coral reefs. If you need to relax, *Yoga Shack (Secret Garden | Jungutbatu | tel. 0813 53 13 68 61 | www.yogashacklembongan. com),* offers daily classes in its bamboo hut. The best way to explore the island is to hire a bicycle or moped from the place where you are staying.

## BEACHES

Swimmers and surfers share the beach with seaweed farmers and fishermen in Jungutbatu. A steep path starting at

## WHERE TO STAY

**INSIDER TIP ▶ CASTAWAY**
Tastefully furnished villa resort, only 200 m/256 ft from the beach. Pool, massage and dining service. *5 villas, 8 suites | Mushroom Bay | tel. 0822 36 90 18 56 | Moderate*

### INDIANA KENANGA
Luxurious boutique hotel with elegant pool and spa and excellent French cuisine. *8 suites | Jungutbatu | tel. 0366 55 93 71 | www.indiana-kenanga-villas. com | Expensive*

### PONDOK BARUNA
One of the oldest hotels on the island with simple, clean rooms, pool and its own diving school. Good beach restau-

rant with friendly service. *22 rooms | Jungutbatu | tel. 0812 3 94 09 92 | www.world-diving.com | Budget*

## WHERE TO GO

### NUSA PENIDA AND NUSA CENINGAN (137 D–F 1–2) *(ω L–N 6–8)*

Very few tourists stay on the larger neighbouring island of *Nusa Penida* but it is a popular destination for snorkelling and diving excursions. Once a prison island, the majority of the inhabitants are Muslims. However, most Balinese avoid the island because of the legend that this is the home of the evil giant Jero Gede Mecaling. Once or twice a year boats from Bali bring offerings on the temple anniversary of the *Pura Dalem Penataran Ped* in *Toyapakeh*, to appease the demon. At the time of the Galungan festival, there is a large procession to the *Goa Karangsari*, an enormous cave 10 km/6.2 mi south of the main town *Sampalan*. The ● *Friends of the National Parks Foundation,* who are active in the protection of wild animals and their natural habitat, operate a *visitor centre (tel. 0828 97 60 86 96 | www.fnpf.org | Budget)* with a simple guesthouse for volunteer helpers in the middle of the bird sanctuary. Public ferries and charter boats depart from Nusa Lembongan for Toyapakeh.

Between Nusa Lembongan and Penida is the small island of *Nusa Ceningan* which can be reached on foot or by bicycle or moped over a narrow bridge from Nusa Lembongan. This is where the first cafés and resorts opened in 2009, including INSIDER TIP *Le Pirate Beach Club (10 bungalows | tel. 0361 48 72 40 | lepirate.com/nusa-ceningan | Budget)*, which also has a restaurant. A walk to the ≈ *Blue Lagoon* at the southern tip is rewarded with spectacular views of the ocean.

# PADANG BAI

(136 C6) *(ω M5)* **For most tourists, the fishing village Bai (pop. 20,000) is merely a stopping-off place on their way to Lombok or the Gilis.**

The main bay is indeed dominated by the ferry terminals but there are also guests who spend their entire holiday here. This is mainly due to the laid-back atmosphere and reasonably priced accommodation, as well as the outstanding diving sites: the coral reefs just off the coast and the islands of Nusa Penida and Nusa Ceningan in the south guarantee spectacular encounters with the colourful life underwater.

## FOOD & DRINK

### OZONE CAFE

A time-honoured institution that is popular with travellers and the locals alike. The cool drinks are accompanied by pizza and live music. *Jl. Segara | tel. 0363 4 15 01 | Budget*

### TOPI INN

This cosy café serves breakfast with muesli, homemade cakes and a Balinese buffet and seafood in the evening. Reading and games corner. *Jl. Silayukti 99 | tel. 0363 4 14 24 | www.topiinn.nl | Budget*

## SPORTS & ACTIVITIES

Padang Bai is one of Bali's most important starting points for diving tours. There are numerous enterprises on the main beach offering courses; the diving school *Paradise Diving Indonesia (Jl. Silayukti 9 Bi | tel. 0811 39 35 15 | www.b-a-l-i.com/english.htm)* and *Water Worx (Jl. Silayukti | tel. 0363 4 12 20 | www.waterworxbali.com)* are recommended. Fishing tours in a traditional boat are the speciality of *Pak Lulu* *(tel. 0813 37 76 80 77).*

## BEACHES

You will be more tempted to just watch the ferries and diving boats at the main beach in Padang Bai than to go for a swim there, two nice swimming and snorkelling beaches are *Blue Lagoon Beach* on the other side of the hill to the east of the main beach, as well as the 'small beach' *Bias Tugal,* which is usually called *White Sand Beach* and is a 15-minute walk along a footpath along the hill west of the ferry port (be careful: the currents here are very strong!).

## WHERE TO STAY

### BLOO LAGOON VILLAGE 🌿 ⊛
Eco-resort catering to families, right above Blue Lagoon Beach; spacious villas, pool, spa and organic restaurant. *24 villas | tel. 0363 4 12 11 | www.bloolagoon. com | Expensive*

### INSIDER TIP▶ DEWI VILLA
Very clean, inexpensive travellers' accommodation with a pool on a hill at the entrance to the town. The friendly staff also offers a shuffle service. *10 rooms | Jl. Raya Padangbai, km 1,1 | tel. 0813 38 62 97 77 | Budget*

### OK DIVERS RESORT
This chic, Colonial-style resort has a pool, a spa and an extremely popular restaurant bar. *30 rooms | Jl. Silayukti 6 | tel. 0811 3 85 88 25 | www.okdiversresort. com | Moderate*

## WHERE TO GO

### GOA LAWAH (136 C6) (*𝄞 M5*)
The 'Bat Cave' with one of the six most sacred temples on Bali is only 5 km/3.1 mi west of Padang Bai. At dusk, the bats leave the cave with a deafening noise. The cave – like the temple – is covered with a thick coating of their excrement. *Daily 8am–6pm | entrance fee 15,000 Rp.*

### KLUNGKUNG (SEMARAPURA) (136 B6) (*𝄞 L5*)
This market town (16 km/9.9 mi) with a population of 57,000 was once the main residence of the first Hindu kings of Bali. When the successor to the throne of the powerful Majapahit Empire was forced to flee in 15th century from the Muslim conquerors of Java, he settled in Gelgel near Klungkung and proclaimed himself ruler of Bali. In 1710, the Gelgel dynasty moved their seat to Klungkung. The only remains of the former glory are a palace gate, the old court hall Kerta Gosa and the Bale Kembang ('floating pavilion'), which can be visited today at the *Taman Gili (daily 8am–6pm | entrance fee 12,000 Rp).* The *Kerta Gosa* in particular, with its elaborate *wayang* style ceiling paintings, is very impressive: judgement was pronounced here, beneath depictions of heavenly pleasures and hellish punishments, until 1950. The larger *Bale Kembang* most recently served as the court's waiting room. The frescoes depict scenes from myths and legends, as well as Balinese everyday life in times gone by. The rest of the palace was destroyed during the Dutch conquest in 1908. The *Puputan Monument* in front of the complex commemorates the entire court's ritual suicide to avoid colonisation. The *Semarajaya Museum* – which documents the history, as well as everyday life to the present day – is also part of the Taman Gili. In 2010, the artist *Nyoman Gunarsa* opened the *museum* named after him *(daily 9am–5pm | entrance fee 25,000 Rp | Jl. Petigaan Banda 1 | Takmung),* which is one of the largest art museums on Bali,

View from the Kerta Gosa to Bale Kembang in Klungkung

3 km/1.9 mi to the west of Klungkung. His studio is also within the museum.

# PEMUTERAN

**(132–133 C–D2)** *(⌖ C2)* **The fishing villa-ge at the north-western tip of Bali, on the edge of the West Bali National Park, has developed into an exclusive destination for snorkellers, divers and nature lovers.** Most of the establishments on the peaceful beaches are upscale resorts with full service: almost every hotel has a restaurant, a spa, its own diving school and organises tours to the national park. There are some less expensive homestays in the village itself. The world's largest project for establishing artificial coral reefs is off the coast of Pemuteran. The village inhabitants, the hotel owners and scientists work hand in hand on the project, which has proven very successful. The *Reef Seen Aquatics (tel. 0362 9 30 01 / www.reefseen.com)* diving centre also operates a turtle station.

## FOOD & DRINK

**INSIDER TIP CAFÉ BALI BALANCE** ⊘
On offer are homemade whole-wheat bread and delicious cakes, fresh fruit juices and salads – and the profits go to a local school project. *Jl. Raya Singaraja-Gilimanuk | Banyupoh | tel. 0853 37 45 54 54 | www.bali-balance.com | Budget*

## WHERE TO STAY

**MATAHARI BEACH RESORT** ⊘
Luxury hotel complex in a fabulous location on the beach, with an award-winning restaurant, excellent spa, pool and numerous leisure activities. The hotel supports a number of social projects that aid the children and elderly in the village. *32 rooms | tel. 0362 9 23 12 | www.matahari-beach-resort.com | Expensive*

**INSIDER TIP THE MENJANGAN** ⊘
This eco-resort with a pool, spa and panoramic restaurant – all built using natural materials and designed to fit into the

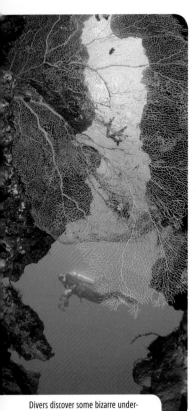

Divers discover some bizarre under-water worlds off Bali's northwest coast

surroundings – has an idyllic location between mangroves and the jungle. Excellent variety of tours. *23 bungalows | Jl. Raya Gilimanuk-Singaraja km 17 | Desa Pejarakan | tel. 0362 9 47 00 | www.the menjangan.com | Expensive*

### PONDOK SARI BEACH RESORT
The 35 bungalows with open-air baths – the water is processed in an environmentally friendly way – restaurant, pool and diving school are scattered through a beautiful garden with lotus ponds. *tel. 0362 9 47 38 | www.pondoksari.com | Moderate*

### SUKASARI HOMESTAY
Family-run bungalow complex, three minutes from the beach, authentic restaurant and lovely garden. *6 rooms | tel. 0813 38 26 28 29 | sukasaripermuteran. com | Budget*

## WHERE TO GO

### PULAU MENJANGAN ★
(132 B1) (*ⅅ B1*)
The uninhabited island off the northwest tip of the national park is considered Bali's best diving area, with an exceptional diversity of coral and fish. Experts will be delighted at the precipitous reefs and a shipwreck while the coral protection project near the beach guarantees enjoyment for beginners and snorkellers. The island is also the site of what is said to be Bali's oldest temple (still preserved in its original state) the *Pura Gili Kencana*; it was supposedly built in the 14th century at a time when the Javanese Majapahit Empire still controlled large sections of what is now Indonesia.

### PURA AGUNG PULAKI (133 D2) (*ⅅ C2*)
The temple on the coast, 5 km/3.1 mi west of Permuteran was rebuilt in 1983 against a dramatic backdrop of cliffs and jungle and commemorates the arrival of the Javanese Hindu priest Nirartha on Bali in the 16th century. The Pura Agung Pulaki is surrounded by three additional temples and is now notorious for the hordes of monkeys that live there as guards. *Daily 8am–6pm | entrance for a donation*

### TAMAN NASIONAL BALI BARAT
(132–133 A–F 2–5) (*ⅅ A–F 2–4*)
25 km/15.5 mi away, in the West Bali National Park covers an area of over 47,000 acres from the coral reefs in

the northwest, the mangroves and arid stretches, to mountain forests on the slopes of volcanoes. 160 different bird species – some of them very rare – live here in addition to monkeys, wild buffaloes, dwarf deer, monitor lizards and snakes. It is possible to drive through the park on your own initiative if you stay on the main road or if you just want to go snorkelling at the beach. However, you have to make use of the services of a registered guide for jeep, boat and trekking tours *(entrance fee 200,000 Rp)*. Most of the treks start from the visitor centre in *Labuhan Lalang,* which is also the point of departure for boats to Pulau Menjangan.

# SANUR

(139 D4) *(*ⓜ *J–K 6–7)* **Sanur (pop. 40,000) is Kuta's more tranquil counterpart and is ideal for a family holiday.**
The sea is calm and so shallow that children can splash around in it; however, it is only possible to swim at high tide. There is a paved path lined with beach bars and cafés all the way along the seaside with the lush gardens of the hotel complexes with their pools behind it. The only high-rise building on Bali was built in the north; today it houses the Inna Grand Bali Beach Hotel. After its construction the government luckily forbade any further high-rise buildings. There are many lovely shops and good restaurants on long *Jl. Danau Tamblingan*. The spectacular *Kite Festival* in the north of Sanur attracts a great number of visitors every year in June/July, as does the *Sanur Village Festival* with art markets, traditional performances, music and water sports activities, which takes place in August.

## SIGHTSEEING

### MUSEUM LE MAYEUR
The Belgian artist Adrien-Jean Le Mayeur – 'Indonesia's Gauguin'– lived in Bali from 1932 until shortly before his death in the year 1958. The museum in the house he once lived displays his work, with many portraits of his wife Ni Pollock, a dancer. The museum shop sells art and handicrafts *Mon–Sat 9am–3pm | entrance fee 20,000 Rp | on the beach path near Jl. Hang Tuah*

## FOOD & DRINK

### CAFE BATU JIMBAR ⊛
Fresh juices, homemade cakes and vegetarian dishes are served in a simple, design atmosphere; organic market on Sunday. *Jl. Danau Tamblingan 75A | tel. 0361 28 73 74 | Moderate*

### RISTORANTE MASSIMO
Classic Italian restaurant that is a perennial favourite: very good pizza, *antipasti* and *gelati*; perfect service. *Jl. Danau Tamblingan 206 | tel. 0361 28 89 42 | Moderate*

### PREGINA
Simple, but tastefully decorated, restaurant serving excellent Balinese dishes at reasonable prices. *Jl. Danau Tamblingan 106 | tel. 0361 28 33 53 | Budget*

### INSIDER TIP WARUNG SANTAI ⊛
This small, friendly bistro serves organic dishes with three different types of rice, as well as tasty wraps, salads and cakes. *Jl. Danau Tandakan 9 | Sindhu | tel. 0361 27 13 90 | Budget*

## SHOPPING

The entire path along the seaside is lined with souvenir shops.

# SANUR

**INSIDERTIP FORUM FAIR TRADE INDONESIA**

Crafts, recycled products and local organic food to Fair Trade standards. *Jl. Bypass Ngurah Rai | Sanur Kaja | forumfairtrade indonesia.org*

## MANIK ORGANIK

This is the place to stock up on organic food, natural cosmetics and bags made from recycled materials, as well as yoga and meditation accessories. Environmental organisations also hold breakfast meetings here. *Jl. Danau Tamblingan 85 | www.manikorganikbali.com*

## NOGO BALI

Clothes, decorations and accessories made from hand-woven cotton fabric, which can also be made according to the client's wishes as well as antique *ikat. Jl. Danau Tamblingan 104 | www. nogobali.com*

## SUARTI MAESTRO

Bali's 'Silver Queen' Suarti describes her jewellery based on old Indonesian models as 'wearable art'. *Jl. Nusa Indah 88 | www.suarti.com*

## SPORTS & ACTIVITIES

Most places offering accommodation also arrange fishing and snorkelling tours in the south of Bali. The surfing spots near Sanur are not as spectacular as those on the west side of the island. *Crystal Divers (Jl. Danau Tamblingan 168 | tel. 0361 28 67 37 | www.crystal-divers.com)* organises good diving courses. The majority of the large hotels have tennis courts, the *Inna Grand Bali Beach Hotel (Jl. Hang Tuah Sanur | www.innagrand balibeach.com)* even has a nine-hole golf course. The *Jamu Traditional Spa* in the Tandjung Sari Hotel *(Jl. Danau*

*Tamblingan 41 | tel. 0361 28 65 95 | www. jamutraditionalspa.com)* offers relaxing treatments using natural local products. The Bamboo Studio of the *Power of Now Oasis (Jl. Retro Beach | Mercure Resort | tel. 0813 38 31 50 32 | powerof nowoasis.com)* offers yoga classes and meditation sessions.

## ENTERTAINMENT

There are chic cocktail bars in the large hotels and many beach cafés offer live music.

## ARENA PUB & BAR

This restaurant-bar has live sports broadcasts, a quiz on Wednesday night and live music and billiards, and is very popular with many foreigners living on Bali. *Daily noon–1am | Bypass Ngurah Rai 115*

## CASABLANCA

From 9pm, local bands play in this popular bar, which offers a tremendous selection of cocktails. *Daily 11am – 1pm | Jl. Danau Tamblingan 120*

## TKS BAR

Small bar with tremendous themed parties, Asian fusion cuisine, drinks and international DJs. *Daily 4pm–3am | Jl. Danau Toba 11*

## WHERE TO STAY

**INSIDERTIP FLASHBACK'S**

Small, tasteful complex with lovely bungalows and one suite; mini pool and café; five minutes from the beach. *9 rooms | Jl. Danau Tamblingan 106 | tel. 0361 28 16 82 | www.flashbacks-chb.com | Budget–Moderate*

**INSIDERTIP KOLONIAL HOUSE**

Very pretty Colonial-style guesthouse with a large pool. Quiet location only 200 m/656 ft from Mertasari Beach.

*Jl. Sekar Waru 20 | eel. 0361 9 38 12 39 | www.kolonialhouse.com | Budget*

## KLUMPU BALI RESORT

Eight charming bungalows in the style of rice repositories, each with its own kitchen, arranged around a pool and spa in the tropical garden. Five minutes to the beach by bike (available to guests). *Jl. Kesari 16b | tel. 0811 203 04 02 | www.klumpu.com | Moderate*

## PURI SANTRIAN

Comfortable hotel complex with private beach and beach club, pool, spa and excellent restaurant. *182 rooms | Jl. Pantai Sanur | tel. 0361 28 80 09 | www.santrian.com/puri | Moderate–Expensive*

## TANDJUNG SARI

The nostalgic bungalow complex with its ornate décor was one of Bali's first beachfront hotels in the 1960s. Pool, spa, restaurant and reading lounge. *26 Bungalows | Jl. Danau Tamblingan 41 | tel. 0361 28 84 41 | www.tandjungsari hotel.com | Expensive*

## THE ZEN VILLAS

Eleven luxurious holiday villas with their own kitchen and private pool in the centre of Sanur. *Jl. Kesari 2 No. 3 B | Sanur | tel. 0361 28 61 29 | www.thezenvillas.com | Expensive*

## WHERE TO GO

### BALI SAFARI & MARINE PARK
### (139 E3) (ⓜ K6)

The popular safari park 23 km/14.3 mi northeast of Sanur is home to more than 50 species of animals – some of them endangered – including white tigers, Komodo dragons, and Sumatra elephants. The visitors travel through the open zoo, which conforms to international standards, by truck. Water and fun park, restaurant and hotel. *Daily 9am–5pm | entrance fee from 39 US$ | Jl. Bypass. Dr. Ida Bagus Mantra km 19.8 | Gianyar | www.balisafa rimarinepark.com*

### BENOA (138–139 C–D5) (ⓜ J7)

Established by the Dutch, Bali's most important port, Labuhan Benoais, is located

With its palm-fringed beaches, Sanur is the perfect spot for a bathing holiday

south of Sanur. Ships with freight anchor here as do the Pelni passenger ships that call at all parts of Indonesia. This is also the departure point for the speedboats to Nusa Lembongan and the Gilis.

## PULAU SERANGAN
(139 D5) (*℧ J7*)
The island owes its name to the sea

beaches shaded by palm trees and there is a rather inconspicuous temple, the *Pura Sakenan*, in the north. It is the site of processions held at important ceremonies intended to appease the gods of the sea. A bridge connects the island with the belt of mangroves to the south of Sanur; boat trips are operated from *Tanjung Benoa*.

A beach pagoda offers stylish shade on Sanur Beach

turtles that used to come here in great numbers to lay their eggs. Today, you will need a great deal of luck to see one of these endangered animals outside of the ● *Turtle Conservation and Education Center (daily 8am–5pm | donation requested)*, which is supported by the WWF (warning: watch out for poor imitations!) – in spite of a ban, they are still being hunted. The south of the small 180 acre island is lined with secluded

# SEMINYAK

(138 C4) (*℧ H7*) ★ At a time when Kuta was still a village and Denpasar a long way away, the rich and famous built their villas in the rice fields around the village of Seminyak.
Today, the town (official pop. 8000) joins seamlessly with Denpasar's Kerobokan and Canggu suburb in the north, while

the former promenade Jalan Arjuna forms the boundary to Legian. Restaurants and boutiques line the former beach road to the Hotel Oberoi, *Kayu Aya*. However, Seminyak is completely different from Kuta and Legian – here, things are little more chic, exclusive and expensive. The beach and waves are just as beautiful as in Kuta and the beach bars reflect the latest design trends. The construction boom has now also extended to the neighbouring villages of *Petitenget*, *Batubelig* and *Canggu,* the surfers' paradise. But, there are still some resorts amidst the rice fields and the beach is empty enough that one can ride along the drift line on horseback.

## FOOD & DRINK

### INSIDER TIP BIKU ◐
The antique furnishing and cake buffet in the bookshop's teahouse promise a pleasant afternoon. Many dishes are prepared using organic ingredients. *Jl. Raya Petitenget 88 | Kerobokan | tel. 0361 8 57 08 88 | www.bikubali.com | Moderate*

### INSIDER TIP GIPSY FISH
Small, very clean restaurant with a terrific selection of fish dishes on the menu. *Jl. Raya Seminyak 17, Bali Bintang Supermarket Square | tel. 0856 3 71 80 47 | Budget–Moderate*

### LA LUCCIOLA ☼
The airy, two-storey beach restaurant serves brunch and fine Italian cuisine. *Jl. Pura Telaga Waja | Petitenget | tel. 0361 73 08 38 | Expensive*

### MAMASAN
Restaurant and lounge in 1920s style, with excellent Asian set meals prepared by the celebrated chef Will Meyrick.

*Jl. Raya Kerobokan 135 | Kerobokan | tel. 0361 73 94 36 | www.mamasanbali.com | Expensive*

### MERAHPUTIH
Experimental Indonesian cuisine in an elegant ambience. *Jl. Petitenget 100x | Kerobokan | tel. 0361 8 46 59 50 | www.merahputihbali.com | Moderate–Expensive*

## SHOPPING

### DOWN TO EARTH ◐
Organic, vegetarian supermarket with an attached café and restaurant, they also have a delivery service. *Jl. Laksmana 99 | www.downtoearthbali.com*

### JEMME
Jewellery by the British designer Luke Stockley; some inspired by Balinese motifs. Exquisite fusion cuisine in the affiliated restaurant. *Jl. Raya Petitenget 28 | Kerobokan | www.jemmebali.com*

### NILUH DJELANTIK
Well-known Balinese shoe designer who counts Cameron Diaz and Gisele Bündchen among her clients. *Jl. Raya Kerobokan 144 | Kerobokan | www.niluhdjelantik.com*

### SEMINYAK VILLAGE SHOPPING MALL ●
Modern shopping centre with plenty of food and fashion and a good selection of beach and surfing fashions. *Jl. Kayu Jati 8 | www.seminyakvillage.com*

## SPORTS & ACTIVITIES

As is the case in Kuta, almost everything in Seminyak revolves around the beach and surfing. Surf courses can be booked from *Bali Green Surf School (Jl. Drupadi 2 | tel. 0819 99 41 22 | www.baligreensurf.net)*. There are also numerous spa services, pamper yourself with a day in the energy-efficient ◐ **INSIDER TIP** *Eastern Garden Martha Tilaar Spa (Jl. Camplung Tanduk 5a | tel. 0361 73 16 48 | www. marthatilaarspa.com)* with a great variety of Far Eastern therapies and natural products. The impressive ● *Prana Spa (Jl. Kunti 118x | tel. 0361 73 08 40 | pranaspabali.com)* provides exquisite treatments and yoga in a décor straight out of the Arabian Nights: Ayurvedic therapies, Balinese herbal scrubs, reflexology and Turkish steam baths. A little less expensive is the Mediterranean atmosphere of *Bodyworks (Jl. Kayu Jati 2 | Petitenget | tel. 0361 73 33 17 | www.bodyworksbali.com)* with a wide selection of massage and body care therapies.

There are wonderful horseback rides along the beach and through the rice fields in the north of Canggu *(Islands Horse Riding | tel. 0361 8 46 96 16 | www.baliislandhorse.com)*.

## ENTERTAINMENT

### HU'U

Chic restaurant bar in a romantic setting with a pool, international bands and DJs. *Sun–Thu 11.30am–1am, Fri/Sat 11.am–3am | Jl. Laksmana | Petitenget*

### JENJA BALI

Bar with a futuristic interior, amazing cocktails and international DJs. The eponymous restaurant serves delicious treats from the Near East. *Wed–Sat until 4am | Townsquare Suites, Jl. Nakula 18*

# FOR BOOKWORMS AND FILM BUFFS

**Earth Dance** – In her novel, Oka Rusmini tells the tale of three generations of women who love, live and suffer under the caste system in Bali (2007)

**The Art and Culture of Bali** – Standard work on Balinese culture by the Swiss ethnologist Urs Ramseyer (2002)

**Love and Death in Bali** – Vicki Baum's classic novel (2007) describes the events that led to the ritual suicide of the royal court of Bandung in 1906

**A Short History of Bali** – Interesting overview of Bali's history (2004) by the diplomat Robert Pringle

**Cowboys in Paradise** – Director Amit Virmani accompanied the Bali Beach Boys on their constant search for foreign girlfriends (2009)

**Eat, Pray, Love** – Parts of the Hollywood film based on the bestseller by Elizabeth Gilbert, and starring Julia Roberts, were filmed on Bali (2010)

**The Year of Living Dangerously** – The film (1982) adaptation of the novel by Christopher Koch takes place in Indonesia during the political turmoil of a coup to overthrow President Sukarno.

**A House in Bali** – This entertaining memoir by composer Colin McPhee (first published in 1947) is the story of his time in Bali documenting gamelan music and all aspects of life on the island in the colonial era

**Sacred & Secret** – The Swiss filmmaker Basil Gelpke documents the religious and social life on Bali through the eyes of Prince Tjokorda Raka Kerthyasa (2010)

### KU DÉ TA ☼
This design lounge on the beach of the Oberoi Hotel has Australian fusion cuisine, excellent cocktails and cool music. *Daily to midnight | Jl. Kayu Aya 9*

### VILLA BLUBAMBU
Chic homestay with two pools and spa service in a beautiful garden. *4 villas |*

The tropical nights are long in Seminyak's beach bars

### POTATO HEAD ☼
Chic, multi-level beach club in unusual design with gigantic pool bar and two acclaimed restaurants, international bands. *Daily 11am–2am | Jl. Petitenget 51b*

### SINGLE MALT BAR ☼
Something different every night: jazz piano, Ladies' Night or Funky DJ – and the greatest whisky selection on Bali. *Daily until 1am | IZE Hotel | Jl. Kayu Aya | short. travel/bal9*

*Jl. Abimanyu | Gang Melon | Seminyak | tel. 0361 73 21 91 | www.villablubambu. com | Expensive*

### DESA SENI ⊛
Eco-resort surrounded by rice fields with tastefully furnished, antique wooden bungalows, pool, spa and organic restaurant. Also art and yoga courses; ten minutes from the beach. *12 bungalows | Jl. Subak Sari 13 | Pantai Berawa | Canggu | tel. 0361 8 44 63 92 | www.desaseni. com | Moderate–Expensive*

The Taman Ayun shrine is notable for the impressive roof construction

## LUNA2 STUDIOTEL

Ultra-modern beach hotel in the 1960s pop art design. Restaurant, bar, pool, spa, own wine cellar and private cinema. *14 rooms | Jl. Sarinande 22 | tel. 0361 73 04 02 | www.luna2.com | Expensive*

**INSIDER TIP** SERENITY ECO GUEST-HOUSE

Friendly family guesthouse with a philosophy of recycling, permaculture garden, a lovely pool and a yoga studio. *5 rooms, 6 dormitory bunks | Jl. Nelayan | Canggu | tel. 0361 8 46 92 57 | serenityecoguesthouse.com | Budget*

## TONY'S VILLAS & RESORT

Secluded hotel complex near the beach in modern Bali style with restaurant, bar, pool, spa. *40 rooms, 22 bungalows, 9 pool villas | Jl. Petitenget | Kerobokan | tel. 0361 4 73 89 17 | www.balitonys.com | Expensive*

## WHERE TO GO

**BALI BIRD PARK** (139 D3) (*∅ J6*)

250 different species of exotic birds flutter around in Bali's bird park around 25 km/15.5 mi northeast of Seminyak. A jungle-like reptile park with snakes, lizards and Komodo dragons is integrated into it. *Daily 9am–5.30pm | entrance fee 32.50 US$ | Jl. Serma Cok Ngurah Gambir Singapadu | Batubulan | www.bali-bird-park.com*

**GUNUNG BATUKARU** ★
(134–135 C–D4) (*∅ G–H 3–4*)

Bali's second highest volcano (2276 m/7467 ft) is considered the island's 'rice basket'. When the weather is clear, you can see as far as the ocean from the spectacular ⚡ *Jatiluwih rice terraces* on the south side. The *Pura Luhur Batukaru* (daily 6am–6pm | entrance fee 20,000 Rp), one of the six holiest temples, lies to the west at an altitude of 825 m/2707 ft about 50 km/31.1 mi from Seminyak. The origins of the enchanted complex, hidden in the forest, date back to the 11th century. It is said a Hindu priest from Java founded the temple here to honour the spirits of the Bratan, Buyan and Tamblingan lakes. A seven-tiered shrine is dedicated to the mountain god Maha Dewa. Today, the complex functions as the ancestral temple of the court of Tabanan. Those who want to explore the mountain in more detail can spend the night in the ⓦ INSIDERTIP *Sarinbuana Eco Lodge (5 bungalows | tel. 0828 97006079 | baliecolodge.com | Moderate)*.

## MENGWI (138 C2) (*J5*)

In 1634, the King of Mengwi had the *Pura Taman Ayun* built as the family sanctuary and it is the second largest temple complex in Bali. It is around 25 km/15.5 mi north of Seminyak in a beautiful, spacious garden surrounded by a moat full of lotus flowers. The water temple is the centrepiece of the sophisticated *subak* system that irrigates the rice fields in Bali. The traditional system is both democratic and ecologically sustainable. A bridge leads to the split entrance gate of the temple. The innermost of the three courtyards can only be entered when important ceremonies are being held but it is possible to get a glimpse of the holy shrines by looking over the outer wall. *Daily 8am–5pm | entrance fee 15,000 Rp.*

## NEGARA (132 C4–5) (*C3–4*)

Negara, the capital city of Jembrana (pop. 80,000, around 100 km/62 mi west of Seminyak), is the most sparsely populated region on Bali, and is mainly known for the buffalo races *(mekepung)* that are held there during the dry season. The region has little in the way of tourist infrastructure, except at the beach at *Medewi,* which is a good surf spot.

## PURA TANAH LOT (138 B3) (*H6*)

Hundred of cameras can be heard clicking when the sun sinks behind the picturesque seaside temple Tanah Lot (15 km/9.3 mi northwest). This is Bali's most popular scene. As can be expected, there are also countless hawkers and guides along the path from the car park to the rock where the temple is located and visitors will have to run the gauntlet to get there. However, if you come to the sacred spot in the early morning, you will really be able to enjoy it. In a cavern beneath the rock, sea snakes, which are revered as sacred, guard the temple against evil. *Daily 7am–7pm | entrance fee 30,000 Rp.*

## TABANAN (138 B2) (*H5*)

The small town 35 km/21.8 mi northwest of Seminyak is home to Bali's *Subak Museum (daily 8am–5pm | entrance fee 15,000 Rp),* which provides fascinating insights into the cultivation and irrigation of the rice fields. Around 6 km/3.7 mi north of Tabanan there is also a *Butterfly Park (daily 8am–5pm | entrance fee 85,000 Rp),* where hundreds of exotic butterflies flutter about.

# UBUD

(139 D2) (*J–K5*) ★ **The cultural and spiritual centre of Bali (pop. 70,000) lies between lush rice terraces and dramatic gorges. As early as the 8th century the Campuan area was declared a holy place by Buddhist monks.**

A branch of the Sukawati dynasty settled in Ubud in the 19th century and built a palace here. In the 1930s Prince Cokorda Gede Agung Sukawati, together with the German Walter Spies and Dutchman Rudolf Bonnet, founded the famous Pita Maha School of Painting here and the movement later paved the way for Western artists and intellectuals thereby helping the local art scene to achieve the extraordinary importance it has to this day.

Spiritual tourism is a somewhat more recent development: yoga and meditation courses are offered on almost every corner and organic food and drink are now a matter of course. Once a year, at the time of the *Bali Spirit Festival (www.bali spiritfestival.com),* Ubud is transformed into an international yoga camp with lots of dancing and music.

Today, the neighbouring villages from *Campuan* to *Tebesaya* have long become integrated into Ubud. There is an almost endless row of shops, restaurants and hotels along long *Jl. Monkey Forest* and, in spite of being so narrow, the traffic creates the feeling of being in a large city. However, not far away, people out for a walk will come across lush rice fields, rushing rivers and forests to gladden any nature lover's heart.

## SIGHTSEEING

### AGUNG RAI MUSEUM OF ART (ARMA)
This museum in a lovely park exhibits works by Balinese artists, Spies, Bonnet, Le Mayeur and the famous Javanese

> **CITY** **WHERE TO START?**
> **Junction in front of Ubud Palace:** this is the heart of Ubud and also the site of the market and central tourist office. Jl. Monkey Forest leads south past countless boutiques and cafés until it reaches the Monkey Forest itself. Take Jl. Ubud Raya to the west and after about 100 m/328 ft you will reach the Puri Lukisan, the Blanco Museum (a further 800 m/2625 ft) and the Neka Museum after just 1 km/0.6 mi further.

painter Affandi. Charming café ● and various courses for tourists. *Daily 9am–6pm | entrance fee 80,000 Rp | Jl. Pengosekan | www.armabali.com*

### THE BLANCO MUSEUM
The eccentric paintings of the Spanish-Philippine artist Antonio Blanco, who died in 1999, can be admired in his palace-like private residence. As in Blanco's art, the building's architecture and furnishings combine European and Balinese elements. *Daily 9am–5pm | entrance fee 80,000 Rp | Jl. Raya Campuan (directly behind the bridge) | www.blancomuseum.com*

# VOLCANOES

There are 128 active volcanoes in Indonesia and 65 of them are considered dangerous. The more than 17,000 islands of the archipelago lie like a string of pearls on the Pacific Ring of Fire where three tectonic plates collide, often resulting in earthquakes. The highest mountain on Bali, the Gunung Agung 3148 m/10,328 ft was believed to be extinct but erupted most recently in 1963 killing over a thousand people. The smaller Gunung Batur is also still active. The Gunung Rinjani (3726 m/12,224 ft) on Lombok is the second highest volcano in the country. Nobody was injured when it last erupted in 2015.

The *Komaneka Gallery (Monkey Forest Road | gallery.komaneka.com)* and the *Tony Raka Art Gallery (Jl. Raya Mas |*

snakes entwined around its body, rests in the door to the inner courtyard. *Daily 8.30am–6pm | entrance fee 40,000 Rp | www.monkeyforestubud.com*

Art is displayed at the Agung Rai Museum, and new works are created there

*www.tonyrakaartgallery.com)* are focused on modern artists from Bali and Java. Contemporary Indonesian and international art is displayed – and can be bought – in *Gaya Fusion (Jl. Raya Sayan | www.gayafusion.com)* and *Sika Gallery (Jl. Raya Campuan | www.sika gallery.com).*

## MONKEY FOREST

Around 300 long-tailed monkeys live in a sacred forest, where they cheekily demand food from the visitors. There are three temples here: a small bathing temple and a cremation temple *(Pura Prajapati)*, as well as the larger *Pura Dalem Agung*, which is guarded by seven figures of witches. A giant stone turtle, with

## NEKA ART MUSEUM

The collection of the art patron Suteja Neka provides an excellent overview of modern Balinese art, as well as works by the Dutchmen Rudolf Bonnet and Arie Smit. *Mon–Sat 9am–5pm, Sun noon–5pm | entrance fee 75,000 Rp | Jl. Raya | Campuan/Kedewatan | www.museum neka.com*

## PURI LUKISAN

A bridge leads into the lush green park of this 'Painting Palace' that was opened in 1953. Works in the old *wayang* style, as well as by young artists and the Pita Maha school of Rudolf Bonnet and Walter Spies, are displayed in several buildings. In addition, there

Apart from the monkeys in the Monkey Forest, you can also admire 115 tree species

are works by contemporary Balinese artists and the famous I Gusti Nyoman Lempad. *Daily 9am–6pm | entrance fee 85,000 Rp | Jl. Raya Ubud | www. museumpurilukisan.com*

### PURI SAREN (UBUD PALACE)

Ubud Palace, which is still the home of the descendants of the last king, is located at the central junction of town. There are several beautifully decorated buildings from the 19th century in the

well maintained garden and dance performances are held in the main courtyard in the evening. *Daily 8am–6pm, performance daily 7.30pm| free admission, dance 80,000 Rp*

## FOOD & DRINK

### ALCHEMY

Raw food, not only for vegans. Various salads, juices and desserts. *Jl. Penestanan Kelod 75 (turn off behind the Blanco Museum) | tel. 0361 97 19 81 | Moderate*

### KAFE@BALISPIRIT

Organic café with an extensive breakfast menu, delicious cakes and salads, as well as yoga courses. Novel furnishing and fittings made using recycled materials. *Jl. Hanoman 44 B | tel. 0361 4 79 20 78 | Budget–Moderate*

### MELTING WOK WARUNG

A French Laotian couple treats diners to cheap Southeast Asian meals in a simple setting. *Jl. Gootama 13 | tel. 0361 9 29 97 16 | Budget–Moderate*

### MOZAIC

One of Bali's best restaurants: chef Chris Salans previously worked in New York and creates multi-course set meals every evening. *Jl. Raya Sanggingan | Campuan | tel. 0361 97 57 68 | Expensive*

### SARI ORGANIK BODAG MALIAH

Freshly-pressed juice and crispy salads are served amidst the rice fields of the Sari Organik permaculture farm. Twenty minutes walk from the centre of town; pick-up service. *Subak Sok Wayah | tel. 0361 97 20 87 | Budget–Moderate*

### INSIDER TIP SENIMAN COFFEE STUDIO

Coffee ground on the premises and – served until the evening – the best breakfast menu in town, as well as barista courses and its own designer products. *Jl. Sriwedari 5 | tel. 0812 36 07 66 40 | Budget–Moderate*

## TUT MAK

This is a popular restaurant with Mediterranean cooking, delicious lunch specials and excellent coffee. *Jl. Dewi Sita (next to the football pitch) | tel. 0361 97 57 54 | Moderate*

## SHOPPING

Ubud has a wealth of boutiques and souvenir shops. You can buy everything you need – from groceries to souvenirs – every day at the *Pasar Ubud (junction of Jl. Raya Ubud/Monkey Forest Road)*. Be sure to use all your bargaining skills! An ☘ organic farmers' market is held every Saturday in front of *Pizza Bagus (10am–2pm | Jl. Raya Pengosekan)*.

There are many villages where handicrafts are produced in the area around Ubud: *Mas* is renowned for its woodcarvers, *Penestanan* for paintings and *Peliatan* for shadow theatre marionettes. The best stonemasons work a little further away in *Batubulan* and *Celuk* is the place to go to buy reasonably-priced silver items.

## BALI BUDA ☘

Popular organic food shop with its own bakery, café and delivery service that supports a number of social projects. *Jl. Jembawan 1 | www.balibuda.com*

## INSIDER TIP EGO SHOP

This small shop in the Sika Gallery sells original objects by young artists at good

Poultry is sold in large baskets on the market in Ubud

prices, with items ranging from ashtrays made from recycled glass to pendants made from papier maché. *Jl. Raya Campuan*

### STUDIO PERAK
Novel silver jewellery at reasonable prices; the owners also give silversmith courses. *Jl. Hanoman and Jl. Monkey Forest | www.studioperak.com*

### THREADS OF LIFE ⊕
The fair trade with high-quality, traditional woven fabrics supports the women who make them while also preserving this particular art form in various parts of Indonesia. *Jl. Kajeng 24 | www.threadsoflife.com*

## SPORTS & ACTIVITIES

Ubud is the ideal starting point for tours to explore the surrounding countryside: rice field hikes and bicycle tours are organised by *Bali Budaya Tours (tel. 0361 97 55 57 | www.baliecocycling.com)*. The birdwatching hikes with the ornithologist *Victor Mason (tel. 0361 97 50 09 | www.balibirdwalk.com)* have become legendary and the medicinal herb strolls *(Herbal Walks | tel. 0812 3 81 60 24 | bali-herbalwalk.com)* are also very interesting. Spas are an important part of Ubud: there is a great variety of affordable spa treatments from the *Sang Spa (Jl. Jembawan 13b and Jl. Monkey Forest | tel. 0361 97 65 00 and 9 08 02 45);* ⊕ *Taksu (Jl. Gootama Selatan 35 | tel. 0361 97 14 90 | www.taksuspa.com)* offers a holistic approach and a panoramic view of the jungle. Yoga and meditation courses are offered everywhere; two that can be recommended are the *Yoga Barn (Jl. Pengosekan | Padang Tegal | tel. 0361 97 12 36 | www.theyogabarn.com)* and the small yoga and meditation centre

INSIDER TIP *White Lotus (Jl. Kajeng 23 | tel. 0899 0 13 49 62 | whitelotusyogameditation.wordpress.com)* where it is possible to have a yoga holiday without any kind of group pressure. The ● *ARMA Museum (see p. 66, tel. 0361 97 66 59)* and *Bali Spirit (Jl. Hanoman | tel. 0361 97 09 92 | www.balispirit.com)* organise interesting courses in Balinese dance, gamelan and handicrafts. Dance and music performances are held every evening in and around Ubud; the *Ubud Tourist Information* will provide you with the current events.

## ENTERTAINMENT

### CP LOUNGE
Restaurant, open-air bar and disco in one. Rainbow-hued shots and dancing until the small hours. *Daily 11am–4am | Jl. Monkey Forest*

### LAUGHING BUDDHA BAR
Exotic cocktails, fabulous live bands and a marvellous atmosphere. *Daily 9pm–midnight | Jl. Monkey Forest (opposite Cafe Wayan)*

### XL SHISHA LOUNGE
Relax with a hubble-bubble and drink in the Near East décor, and enjoy the live music from 7.30pm. *Daily 11am–3am | Jl. Monkey Forest 129 (behind the football pitch)*

## WHERE TO STAY

### ALAM INDAH ☙
Bright rooms in Balinese style overlooking the Wo River valley. Pool, spa and quiet garden. *10 rooms | Nyuhkuning | tel. 0361 97 46 29 | www.alamindahbali.com | Moderate*

### CITRUS TREE VILLAS
16 modern, minimalistic rooms and a private villa, 15 minutes from the cen-

tre of town. Pool and breakfast service. *Jl. Sriwedari 14 | tel. 0361 971145 | www. citrustreevillas.com | Budget–Moderate*

### GUCI GUESTHOUSE
Artist homestay in a quiet location with five large bungalows in a beautiful garden, a duplex with kitchen for families. Very friendly service. *Jl. Raya Pengosekan | tel. 0361 97 59 75 | www.guci-bali. com | Budget*

### KAJANE
The luxurious, beautifully landscaped villa resort with pool, natural spa and organic restaurant is in the very heart of town. *40 rooms, 8 villas | Jl. Monkey Forest | tel. 0361 97 28 77 | www.kajane. com | Moderate–Expensive*

### KENANGA BOUTIQUE HOTEL
Chic, contemporary hotel with a fantastic view of the rice terraces outside of Ubud. Restaurant, gigantic pool and spa where you can have treatments with products made on the premises. *21 rooms | Jl. Lungsiakan | tel. 0361 8 98 97 00 | www. kenangaubud.com | Expensive*

### KETUT'S PLACE
Family hotel with lovely garden that overlooks the valley, pool and spa. If requested in advance, the owners will make a delicious Balinese buffet meal. *17 rooms | Jl. Suweta 40 | tel. 0361 97 53 04 | www.ketutsplace.com | Budget–Moderate*

### INSIDER TIP VILLA PECATU
The five modern apartments, each with a large terrace and kitchen, are located right next to a rice field. Shared pool. Very helpful owners. *Jl. Pengosekan (opposite Panorama Hotel) | tel. 0812 3 91 90 87 | villapecatu@hotmail.com | Moderate*

Only guests of the Ketut's Place are able to enjoy this garden idyll

Everyday life at the crater lake in front of the majestic Gunung Batur

### TJAMPUHAN HOTEL ☀

The former home of the painter Walter Spies with a view of a canyon forms part of the elegant, historic hotel that has two swimming pools, a luxurious spa and a fancy restaurant. Original works by the artist Walter Spies are on display in the lounge that bears his name. *67 rooms | Jl. Raya Campuan | tel. 036197 53 68 | www.tjampuhan-bali.com | Expensive*

## INFORMATION

### UBUD TOURIST INFORMATION
*Jl. Raya Ubud (opposite Ubud Palace) | tel. 0361 97 32 85*

## WHERE TO GO

### GOA GAJAH ☀ (139 D2) (*M K5*)
Southeast of Ubud (2 km/1.2 mi) steep steps leads up to the so-called Elephant Cave from the 9th century. One enters the interior with a statue of the god Ganesha – depicted as half man, half elephant – through the mouth of a demon. The Dutch came across the cave in 1923 and the sacred spring with the two rectangular bathing places in front of it was discovered 30 years later. You should try to arrive here as early as possible in order to avoid the tour groups. *Daily 8am–5pm | entrance fee 15,000 Rp.*

### GUNUNG BATUR ★ ☀
(136 A–B 2–3) (*M L2–3*)
If you want to experience sunrise on the summit of the Gunung Batur (1717 m/ 5633 ft, 45 km/28 mi northeast), you will have to get up early in the morning and climb in the dark up a stony path for around two hours – but it is well worth the effort as the view over the volcanic

landscape is breathtaking. There are several routes and tours are arranged by *Bali Budaya Tours (tel. 0361 97 55 57 | www.baliecocycling.com)* and other organisations.

The view from ☀ *Penelokan* (around 30 km/18.6 mi north of Ubud) is no less impressive and getting there is considerably less strenuous. With a length of 8 km/5 mi, Bali's largest crater lake *Danau Batur* takes up about one third of the inner caldera 500 m/1640 ft below the crater rim. The *Pura Ulun Danu Batur* temple is dedicated to the goddess of the lake and was moved from the northern edge to a higher location after an earthquake in 1926.

The Bali Aga village *Trunyan,* on the eastern side can be reached by boat from Kedisan. The people living there do not bury their dead but lay them out under bamboo frames in the cemetery. They are suspicious of strangers and it is advisable to only visit in the company of a good guide.

## GUNUNG KAWI ☀ (139 E1) (*ⓜ K4*)

A stairway hewn into the rocks leads into a fertile valley 20 km/12.4 mi north of Ubud. Here, you will discover nine 7 m/23 ft high niches in the rocks with carved shrines that supposedly date back to the 11th century. It is believed that the tombs of King Anak Wungsu and his family are behind them. According to the legend, the giant Kebo Iwa scratched them out of the rock. There is a tenth statue further down on the other side of the river where a former Buddhist monastery is also located. *Daily 8am–5pm | entrance fee 15,000 Rp.*

## PEJENG (139 D2) (*ⓜ K5*)

One of Bali's six holiest temples, the *Pura Pusering Jagat* ('Temple at the Navel of the World'), where mainly young couples pray to be blessed with offspring, lies exactly in the middle of Bali at the centre of the old Pejeng Empire, 3 km/1.9 mi east of Ubud. 300 m/984 ft further on, you can see the world's largest bronze drum and most important find from the Indonesian Bronze Age, the 'Moon of Pejeng', in the *Pura Penataran Sasih*. The nearby archaeological museum, *Gedung Arca Museum Arkeologi (Mon–Fri 8am–4pm | free admission),* has a display of artefacts that are over 2000 years old, diagonally across from the *Pura Kebo Edan*, the 'Temple of the Mad Buffalo', that is famous for a 3.6 m/11.8 ft high statue of Shiva. Today, the descendants of the king run a batik manufacture in the old palace *Puri Pejeng* to support the village (⚫ INSIDER TIP *BISA Organic Batik | tel. 0813 37 33 09 44)*, as well as an idyllic ⚫ INSIDER TIP *organic farm (Kebun Setaman Pejeng | tel. 0813 29 31 97 77)* that offers courses in permaculture.

## TIRTA EMPUL (139 E1) (*ⓜ K4*)

The Balinese have made pilgrimages to the sacred springs (25 km/15.5 mi north of Ubud), which – it is said – the Hindu god Indra invested with magical powers, for more than 1000 years. The clear water bubbles out of twelve carved fountains into the main pool and there are two smaller pools fed by the spring further down. *Daily 8am–5pm | entrance fee 15,000 Rp.*

## YEH PULU (139 D2) (*ⓜ K5*)

A path along a brook leads to the *stone reliefs* near a sacred spring 2 km/1.2 mi to the east of Ubud. The reliefs from the 14th century were discovered in 1925 but there is still some uncertainty over their meaning.

# LOMBOK

For a long time, Lombok was over-shadowed by its neighbouring island Bali, but now an increasing number of tourists have become interested in what is one of Indonesia's most fascinating islands: this is where Islam and Hinduism meet, where traditional and modern life rub shoulders, and where tropical rainforests and Austronesia savannahs merge.

Lombok (Indonesian for 'chilli') is dominated by the majestic massif of the 3726 m/12,224 ft high volcano Mount Rinjani, which covers the northern half of the island. Here, fertile rice terraces, palm groves and forests populated by monkeys and other wild animals extend up the steep mountain slopes. The gigantic crater lake is held sacred by both the Muslim Sasak, Lombok's indigenous population, and Balinese Hindus and is one of the main attractions for tourists. In the arid south picturesque bays and coral reefs (with perfect conditions for surfers and divers) lie hidden between cliffs in front of the hilly savannah landscape. The 1824 mi$^2$ large island has the Wallace Line to thank for its overwhelming biodiversity: the border between the Asian and Australian primeval continent ran through the 40 km/24.9 mi wide and up to 3000 m/9843 ft deep ocean trench between Lombok and Bali. The flora and fauna of Southeast Asia and Austronesia mixed here over thousands of years.

Lombok is more unspoilt, more natural than Bali; but, it is also harsher. The about 3.5 million inhabitants live main-

Island of great diversity: luxuriant nature and cultural contrasts make Lombok a fascinating travel destination for explorers

ly from agriculture and only the western and southern section of the island have been really developed for tourism. The Sasak people are devout Muslims, they value modesty and have conservative views about alcohol consumption, especially outside of the tourist resorts. The villages in the east, in particular, are often dominated by outsized mosques. In spite of that, Hindu and animist customs have found their way into Islam as it is practiced here – especially by the followers of the Wetu Telu faith ('three elements') in the north of the island who see themselves as the descendants of the first Islamic preacher on Lombok. They only pray three times a day and fast for a mere three days during Ramadan. However, out of fear of being discriminated against, very few openly profess their faith. A Hindu minority lives in the west; they are the descendants of the Balinese rulers who conquered Lombok in the 17th century before being driven out themselves by the Dutch at the end on the 19th century. Some temples and

Lombok's mountains are still home to villages that have not been discovered by tourists

palaces around the capital city Mataram still bear witness to this period.

Lombok was considered an insider tip for a long time. However, with the opening of the new international airport only a few miles north of Kuta a new wave of tourism – promoted by the government campaign 'Visit Lombok Sumbawa' – started on the island. As the coast around Senggigi is mostly developed, investors are now focusing on the south of the island. The Mandalika Resort Project, a vast and exclusive holiday park with international 5-star hotels and villa estates, is to reach from Kuta to Gerupuk. The first resorts will open in 2018. In spite of that, Lombok – with its huge mountains, countless bays and dozens of lesser-known *gilis* ('small islands') – has remained a paradise for tourists who want to discover new places.

# KUTA

(140 C5) (*ɲ R9*) **Unlike Bali's Kuta, this small fishing village on the south coast of Lombok is rather peaceful. This place is particularly attractive in the twilight, as the shrimpers set out with their nets, their lamps bathing the entire bay in a romantic light.**

All of the cafés and shops along the long beach had to move under an initiative by the villagers so it remained accessible by all. The hotels and restaurants now all line the main street. They are used primarily by backpackers and surfers, who value Kuta as the perfect starting point for exploring the spectacular ★ *south-coast of Lombok*: the coast road winds its way past wild hills and rugged cliffs with still more beautiful bays and secluded beaches, the further one travels. With the exception of some moped riders and taxi drivers, the only people on the road are some farmers in their buffalo-drawn wagons; some of them still live in traditional Sasak villages such as *Rambitan* and *Sade* in the south. At the time of the full moon in February/March, they all congregate on Kuta's beaches to celebrate the Bau Nyale Festival when they catch Nyale worms between the coral and then fry and eat them. There is also a great deal of flirting at this fertility ritual.

## FOOD & DRINK

Most of the places offering accommodation in and around Kuta also have a café or restaurant.

### ASHTARI ● ⬝

Popular restaurant with lounge atmosphere located on a hill to the west of Kuta with a fantastic view of the bay. *Daily | Jl. Raya Kuta-Mawun | tel. 0877 65 49 76 25 | Moderate–Expensive*

### GULA'S GARDEN BAR

An address for those with a romantic nature, who can enjoy the hearty Western cuisine and very friendly service in the delightful garden. *Jl. Pariwisata (Kuta Cave Hotel) | tel. 0370 6 15 80 80 | Budget–Moderate*

### NUGGETS CORNER

This exclusive *warung* offers a tremendous range of Indonesian dishes as well as a vegetarian menu and fabulous juices. *Jl. Raya Kuta/Ecke Jl. Mawun | tel. 0878 65 46 15 05 | Budget*

## SPORTS & ACTIVITIES

The most popular bays for this sport are *Mawi* in the west and *Gerupuk* and *Tanjung Aan* in the east. *Lombok School of Surf (Jl. Pantai Kuta | tel. 0812 39 32 19 15 | www.lombokschoolofsurfing.com)* organises equipment, courses and tours to more distant surf spots. Diving courses and tours to the less visited, but spectacular, diving spots in the south of Lombok are offered by *Discovery Divers (Jl. Raya Kuta | tel. 0812 52 19 92 72 | www.discoverydiverslombok.com)*.

## BEACHES

Kuta's beach has a beautiful esplanade and offers many local activities, but is

**MARCO POLO HIGHLIGHTS**

★ **Lombok's south coast**
Picturesque bays with white sandy beaches → p. 76

★ **Rambitan and Sade**
Visit these villages for some insights into the lifestyle of Lombok's indigenous people → p. 79

★ **Tetebatu**
Nature and quietude between rice fields, orchards and waterfalls → p. 82

★ **Sekotong**
A paradise for divers in between tiny islets → p. 83

★ **Gunung Rinjani**
Covering almost half the island, the fascinating landscape of the mighty volcano attracts not only climbers → p. 85

★ **Banyumulek and Sukarara**
The two villages are well-known for their handicrafts – and good places to shop → p. 89

not really inviting for bathing. There is an ideal bathing beach 10 km/6.2 mi west of the town in the beautiful curved bay at *Mawun*. Further to the west, follow the road past the surfing beach at *Mawi* until you arrive at the bay at INSIDER TIP *Selong Belanak,* with its breathtaking panorama of the cliffs at sunset. If you want to enjoy this spectacle for longer,

mosphere right at the centre. *Jl. Raya Pantai Kuta | tel. 0370 6 15 80 56 | short. travel/bal10 | Budget*

### NOVOTEL LOMBOK

Sasak style resort 3 km/1.9 mi east of the village that supports a variety of environmental projects. Two pools, a spa, a restaurant, leisure activities and

It's not every day that Kuta's fishermen fill their nets

you can spend the night in the very beautiful *Sempiak Villas (3 villas| tel. 0821 7 44 30 33 37 | www.sempiakvillas.com | Budget)* – or just have a delicious dinner in the complex's *Laut Biru* restaurant. The sheltered sandy beach at *Tanjung Aan* around 7 km/4.4 mi east of Kuta is ideal for swimming and snorkelling. A further 3 km/1.9 mi to the east, you reach *Gerupuk Bay,* which is very popular with surfers.

### WHERE TO STAY

### BOMBORA BUNGALOWS

Eight basic bungalows in the South Seas style, plus a lovely pool and relaxed at-

a picture-perfect beach. *102 rooms | Pantai Putri Nyale | tel. 0370 6 15 33 33 | www.novotel-lombok.com | Expensive*

### PURI RINJANI

Clean, basic bungalows in a tropical garden with a large pool and a café lounge with beach views. *19 rooms | Jl. Raya Pantai Kuta | tel. 0370 6 15 48 49 | the rinjanikutalombok@gmail.com | Budget*

### INSIDER TIP YULI'S HOMESTAY

Spotlessly clean child-friendly facility with eight bungalows and two pools in a beautiful garden; shared kitchen. 15 minutes from the beach. Very pleasant hosts. *Jl. Batu Riti | tel. 0819 17 10 09 83 | www.yulishomestay.com | Budget*

## WHERE TO GO

### EKAS BAY ✻ (141 D–E5) (*𝄐 S9*)
This bay in the southeast of Lombok is hardly developed for tourism, but has some of the island's very best spots for surfing, diving and snorkelling. After leaving Kuta, drive for around 25 km/15.5 mi to the fishing village of Awang and then take a boat to the other side. For a longer stay you can book into the eco-resort 🌐 INSIDER TIP *Heaven on the Planet (17 chalets | tel. 0812 3 75 11 03 | www.sanctuaryinlombok.com | Moderate)* in a spectacular location on the cliffs. An alternative route is over a bumpy road to the east.

### RAMBITAN AND SADE ★
(141 D5) (*𝄐 R–S9*)
The traditional Sasak villages of Rambitan and Sade are just 6 km/3.7 mi north of Kuta. The single-room houses are built of clay and wood and roofed with grass; in between, you will see the rice granaries *(lumbung)* with their low slung, bulbous roofs of palm leaves that have served as models for countless bungalow resorts. Although these two villages cater to tourists, it is still interesting to get an insight into original village life. You should not let them wheedle too much money out of you for souvenirs and the mandatory guide; usually, a single donation at the entrance to the village is enough.

# MATARAM

(140 B3) (*𝄐 Q7*) **Lombok's capital is a conglomeration of four towns that have now merged seamlessly into one and have a population of almost half a mil-** lion residents: the old port of Ampenan, Cakranegara with its Chinese character, the small market town of Sweta, and Mataram itself – a former royal city that is now dominated by.

Some temples and palaces still bear witness to past glory. *Mataram* and *Cakranegara*, with their business and shopping centres, form the bustling centre of the island. The former Dutch commercial port *Ampenan* is mainly used by fishing boats today. A main thoroughfare runs from there as far as *Sweta;* all of the addresses that are of interest to tourists can be found nearby. Most visitors merely pass through the town – but anybody interested in the everyday life in an Indonesian provincial town should make an excursion here.

## SIGHTSEEING

### MAYURA WATER PALACE
The 'floating pavilion' was erected in the middle of a lotus pond in 1744. It served as a court hall during the period of Balinese rule and this was where the Balinese fought against the Dutch at the end of the 19th century. Unfortunately, the remains of the complex were not main-

---

🏙 **WHERE TO START?**
**Mataram Mall:** About 200 m/656 ft after you leave the mall on Jl. Pejanggik you will reach the Rinjani weaving mill on the other side of the street. Turn to the left and after about 500 m/1640 ft you will arrive at the Sindhu market, continue straight ahead to the Pura Meru and Mayura water palace (Jl. Selaparang). Buses leave from here for the Mandalika market at the Sweta bus terminus.

tained for many years and there were no renovations until 2012. The architectural melange of Hindu and Islamic elements, as well as the historical significance of the site – which only becomes clear to the layperson with the help of a knowledgeable guide *(set prices are displayed at the entrance)* – makes the water palace interesting for tourists. *Daily 7am–6pm | entrance fee 10,000 Rp | Jl. Selaparang | Cakranegara*

### MUSEUM NUSA TENGGARA BARAT ●

From wedding dresses, to shadow theatre puppets and daggers: you can learn a great deal about the culture and history of the Nusa Tenggara Barat province – to which Lombok and Sumbawa both belong – here. A translator (your driver or a guide) can be helpful. *Tue–Thu 8am–3pm, Fri 8am–4pm, Sat/Sun 8am–3.30pm | entrance fee 5000 Rp | Jl. Panji Tilar Negara 6 | Mataram*

### PURA MERU ⚞

A Balinese prince had the largest Hindu temple on Lombok built in 1720, in an attempt to unify the island's inhabitants. A path leads through two forecourts to an inner courtyard with 33 shrines. Three *meru* (pagodas), of different heights in a row, are dedicated to the three main Hindu deities Shiva, Brahma and Vishnu. It becomes overcrowded at the Pujawali festival held every year at full moon in October. *Daily 8am–5pm | admission for a donation | Jl. Selaparang | Cakranegara*

## LOW BUDGET

The trip between the new airport, Mataram and Senggigi is much cheaper with the *DAMRI Airport Bus (30,000 Rp)* than by taxi *(200,000 Rp)*. However, the unreliable schedule of the bus makes this only advisable when you arrive.

You can buy authentic souvenirs considerably cheaper on trips to Lombok's *handicraft villages* than at the markets or in shops.

With the exception of Senggigi, wellness treatments are usually limited to spas in the major hotels and are correspondingly expensive. Most places offering accommodation are also able to arrange a private masseur on request (from 100,000 Rp per hour).

## FOOD & DRINK

### INSIDER TIP ▶ LESEHAN TALIWANG IRAMA

This restaurant is popular with the locals for its authentic Sasak cooking; it is said that this is the place to eat the best *Taliwang* chicken on Lombok. *Jl. Ade Irma Suryiani | Gang Salam 6 | Cakranegara | tel. 0370 62 31 63 | Budget*

### ROCK GILIS COFFEE

A popular coffee shop with young Indonesians that serves western snacks and pizzas. *Jl. Langko 23F/G | tel. 0370 64 98 22 | Budget*

## SHOPPING

There are many small antique shops on *Jl. Saleh Sungkar* in Ampenan. Groceries, cosmetics and electrical appliances can be bought in the *Mataram Mall* and at other places. The largest traditional market on Lombok is right next to the Mandalika bus terminus in *Sweta*.

Stone guard in the traditional headdress at Mayura water palace

### LOMBOK EPICENTRUM

The island's first mega mall has four floors with local and international food and fashion outlets and a large cinema complex. *Jl. Sriwijaya (Ex-Bupati Mataram) | www.lombokepicentrum.com*

### LOMBOK SASAKU

T-shirts, bags and other souvenirs with contemporary motifs of Lombok and the Sasak culture. *Jl. Lembar (Kompleks Pertokoan Dasan Cermen 31 & 32) | www.lomboksasaku.com*

## WHERE TO STAY

**INSIDER TIP PONDOK ANGGREK PUTIH**
Very friendly, beautifully looked-after homestay with a pool and a lavish tropical garden, 10-minute drive to Senggigi, excellent cooking courses. *4 rooms | Dusun Presak | Meninting | Mataram | tel. 0821 47 82 00 60 | Budget*

### HOTEL SANTIKA LOMBOK

The most modern business hotel in town with restaurant, bar, pool and gym. *123 rooms | Jl. Pejanggik 32 | Mataram | tel. 0370 6 17 88 88 | www.santika.com/santika-lombok | Moderate*

## INFORMATION

**WEST NUSA TENGGARA TOURISM OFFICE**
*Jl. Singosari 2 | Mataram | tel. 0370 63 17 30*

## WHERE TO GO

### PURA LINGSAR
(140 C3) *(∅ R7)*

A Hindu temple and a Wetu Telu mosque stand peacefully next to each other in the largest temple complex 7 km/4.4 mi east of Cakranegara. The main section was built in 1714. As soon as the rainy season begins, Hindus and Sasak compete in the playful ● *Perang Topat* ('Rice Cake War'). *Daily 7am–6pm | admission for a donation*

## SURANADI
(140 C3) (*📖 R7*)

The refreshing climate in this small town, only 18 km/11.2 mi away from Mataram, makes it a popular place for excursions. The *Pura Suranadi* is the oldest and most important Hindu temple on Lombok. It was supposedly founded in the 16th century by the same Hindu priest who had Bali's six most sacred temples erected. Sacred moray eels swim in the temple spring and there is a flying fox station in the nearby monkey forest. The *Permandian Surandi* from the colonial era is a pool fed with cool spring water *(entrance fee 10,000 Rp)* that is very popular on weekends.

## TAMAN NARMADA (140 C4) (*📖 R7*)

The Narmada Park (11 km/6.8 mi east of Mataram) was laid out in 1727 by the Balinese King Anak Agung Gede Ngurah in honour of the god Shiva. A pleasure garden modelled on the Rinjani volcano was created around the *Pura Kalasa* temple; the large pool represents the crater lake. This made it possible for the king to continue to make his ritual offerings at the sacred water after he had become too old to climb the Rinjani itself. The terrace-like gardens and *public swimming pool (Fri closed | 5000 Rp)* make the spacious complex a popular weekend destination for people from the city. *Daily 7am–6pm | entrance fee 10 000 Rp.*

## TETEBATU ★ ● (141 D3) (*📖 S7*)

This small village at an altitude of 400 m/1312 ft (47 km/29.2 mi from Mataram) is surrounded by rice terraces that are used as tobacco fields in the dry season. The village's panorama and refreshing climate already made it a popular destination for excursions in the colonial era. Today, it is mainly visited by day-trippers and backpackers hiking to the nearby *Joben* and *Jukut* waterfalls (around 2 hours) or just looking for peace and

Head-high tobacco plants in the fields near Tetebatu

quiet. You can spend the night in the *Les Rizières (4 rooms | tel. 0859 03 13 81 11 | www.les-rizieres.com | Budget)*, a guesthouse surrounded by rice fields. The monkey forest close by and orchards where coffee, cocoa, vanilla and cloves grow, are very inviting for long walks. The handicrafts village of *Loyok,* which is famous for its wickerwork, is 10 km/6.2 mi further to the south.

# SEKOTONG

(140 B4) *(ﾘ Q8)* ⭐ **In south-west Lombok is the mountainous peninsula that investors only recently discovered for tourism.**

A winding road weaves its way through small Sasak villages along the north coast with more than a dozen – mostly uninhabited – islands out to sea: the 'secret' Gilis. The islets have white sandy beaches, colourful corals and crystal-clear water and are a paradise for snorkellers and divers. There is a very bumpy road to the extreme western point *Bangko-Bangko,* where the breakers roll to shore at Desert Point, which is so famous amongst surfers. *Teluk Mekaki* is the only accessible bay in the south. Many new resorts have opened on Sekotong and the small Gili Islands in recent years. The people live their traditional lives of agriculture and gold prospecting. A pearl farm is in operation on *Gili Gede*. There are only a few shops; the daily market in *Pelangan* offers food and handicrafts.

## SPORTS & ACTIVITIES

All the resorts organise snorkelling tours and professional diving tours and courses can be booked from *Divezone (tel. 0819 07 85 20 73 | www.divezone-lombok.*

*com). Desert Point* near Bangko-Bangko is considered the best surfing spot on Lombok – some resorts offer trips. If you want to explore the mountains on a bicycle, contact *Mountain Bike Lombok (tel. 0819 99 09 71 26 | www.mountain bikelombok.com).*

## WHERE TO STAY

### COCOTINOS ⊕

Chic boutique resort in a palm grove with a view of the Gilis; pool, spa, restaurant and dive school, natural building design and waste recycling. *36 rooms | Dusun Pandanan | Sekotong Barat | tel. 0819 07 97 24 01 | www.cocotinos-seko tong.com | Budget*

### INSIDER**TIP** PEARL BEACH RESORT

Idyllic island resort at a former pearl farm; restaurant, spa and dive school. *10 bungalows | Gili Asahan | tel. 0819 0 72 47 69 | www.pearlbeach-resort.com | Budget*

### VIA VACARE ⊕

Very friendly, basic eco resort on the largest of the small Gilis that is notable for its local project with plastic recycling, water- and energy-saving programmes. Daily yoga sessions, full board included. *8 rooms | Gili Gede | tel. 0812 37 32 45 65 | Budget–Moderate*

# SENARU

(141 D2) *(ﾘ S6)* **The ⚜ small village on the slopes of the Rinjani is picturesquely nestled between lush rice terrace, flowering gardens and palm groves and is the most important starting point for climbs up the majestic volcano.**

Those who don't want to tackle the multi-day climb to the summit can relax and enjoy the fresh air and fantastic views by undertaking short excursions through the rice fields and rainforests to thundering waterfalls, or become acquainted with the traditional way of life of the villagers.

## SPORTS & ACTIVITIES

Most of the tourists who come to Senaru aim to climb the Rinjani. Depending on the route, the hike takes three to four days and should never be undertaken without a professional guide. The ascent is usually too dangerous during the rainy season – and, of course, this is also true if the volcano is too active. The tours are organised centrally by *Rinjani Trek Ecotourism (Senaru/Senggigi/Sembalun/Mataram | tel. 0370 64 11 24 | www.lombok rinjanitrek.org)* whose office is located at the upper end of Senaru at the entrance to the national park. This is where all of the professional trekking operators that work together with the national park and village administration are registered *(such as John's Adventures | tel. 0817 5 78 80 18 | www.rinjanimaster.com.* Most accommodations in Senaru will help their guests to arrange a hike *(cost: around 4,000,000 Rp per person – the larger the group, the cheaper the price).*

## WHERE TO STAY

Most of the places providing accommodation also have small restaurants.

### RINJANI LIGHT HOUSE ☺
The clean wooden house on stilts offers fresh local food in the adjacent *warung* and supports the women's mountain guide organisation. *4 rooms, 1 family cottage | Jl. Pariwisata Senaru (near the entrance to the national park) | tel. 0818 05 48 54 80 | www.rinjanilighthouse.mm.st | Budget*

### RINJANI LODGE ☆
Fabulous boutique hotel with two pools, a restaurant and fantastic views. *5 rooms | Jl. Raya Senaru | tel. 0819 07 38 49 44 | www.rinjanilodge.com | Moderate*

### INSIDER TIP RINJANI MOUNTAIN GARDEN ☆ ☺
This eco-resort with its luxuriant garden, natural swimming pool and all kinds of animals is located on the eastern side of the Senaru Valley high up on the slopes of the Rinjani. You can enjoy the fantastic views over rice terraces and coconut plantations all the way down to the ocean while savouring a delicious meal of Indonesian and European specialties in the restaurant, as well as undertake trekking and horseback tours. Those who do not want to spend the night in a hired tent can stay in one of the six pretty rice-granary style cottages. The electricity is generated by hydropower. *Teres Genit | Bayan | tel. 0818 56 97 30 | Budget*

## WHERE TO GO

### BAYAN
(141 D2) (*⌀ S6*)
The main village of the Wetu Telu followers is 6 km/3.7 mi north of Senaru is the site of the oldest mosque on the island. Built from bamboo and clay it is 300 years old. The inhabitants of Bayan regard themselves as direct descendants of the holy man who is said to have brought Islam to the island in the 16th century and they have continued to maintain a mixture of animistic, Hindu and Islamic traditions to the present day. For a small donation, the mosque guardian will be delighted to tell you the history of the village. However, you will have to rely on the translation skills of your driver if you want to understand him.

## DUSUN SENARU AND SEGENTER
(141 D1–2) (*∅ S6*)

The unspoilt village of *Senaru* is at the upper end of this vacation spot: the people here still live as they did hundreds of years ago in communal bamboo houses with clay floors but that now also contain a TV and refrigerator. The architectural style, language and traditions differ from those of the Sasak in the south. Visitors in Indonesia and its majestic massif covers around half of the surface of Lombok. The *Segara Anak* ('Child of the Sea') lake in its gigantic crater is up to 6 km/3.7 mi wide and is considered sacred by both the Sasak and Hindus on Lombok. The active *Gunung Baru,* which was created following a powerful eruption of the mother volcano, towers up next to it. Nobody suffered injuries when it last

The turquoise waters of the sacred lake, the Segara Anak, glistening in the crater of the Gunung Rinjani

who make a small donation at the entrance to the village will be shown the traditional way of life and increasingly professional guides. Around 12 km/7.5 mi north on the road to Senggigi, there is a signpost pointing to *Segenter,* another completely preserved Sasak village which is now also a popular destination for travel groups.

## GUNUNG RINJANI ★
(141 D–E2) (*∅ R–T 6–7*)

Its height of 3726 m/12,224 ft makes the Rinjani the second highest volcano erupted in 2015. The ● *Rinjani National Park (entrance fee 150,000 Rp)* covers 101,313 acres of lush rainforest and bizarre volcanic landscapes and is the home of unique flora and fauna: wild boar, dwarf deer and giant lizards, as well as rare birds, butterflies and plants. After you start your ascent at Sena, you will pass caves and hot springs that the local people believe have magical powers. There is an additional entrance to the national park in Sembalun Lawang in the east. On no account should you attempt to climb the mountain on your

### SINDANGGILA AND TIU KELEP WATERFALLS (141 D2) *(𝕄 S6)*

Around 1.5 km/0.9 mi from Senaru the picturesque Sindanggila Waterfall plummets thunderously down into the valley over two cascades. The footpath from the main road *(next to the Pondok Senaru Restaurant | entrance fee 10,000 Rp)* is well developed and the walk takes around 20 minutes. People are usually accompanied by a guide (do not pay more than noted on the sign at the entrance). A real professional is only required if you want to continue your climb up to the Tiu Kelep Waterfall: a steep, slippery path leads to a natural swimming pool in around three quarters of an hour.

# SENGGIGI

**(140 B3) *(𝕄 Q7)* This former fishing village (pop. 5000) in the west of Lombok has now spread out over several beautiful, curved bays – and there is no sign of the building work stopping.**

The white ☀ sand beaches – from where you can see as far as Bali's majestic Gunung Agung at sunset on a clear day – make the place an ideal holiday destination. Of course, the strategic location, between the ferry harbour in Labuhan Lembar, the old airport at Ampenan and the Gilis in the northwest, has also helped Senggigi's development into Lombok's most important tourist destination. This is the perfect starting point to explore Lombok from the land or water.

Although there are restaurants and places offering accommodation in all price categories, Senggigi has remained very peaceful and inexpensive when compared to the tourist centres on Bali.

The Sindanggila Waterfall cascades down from the Gunung Rinjani to the valley

own, the way up is 20 km/12.4 mi long. Despite warning there are always some stubborn tourists who do so and end up getting lost in the wilderness, injure themselves or even perish. The increasing number of trekking tours has led to the introduction of a ♻ zero-waste programme in which the bearers are paid an extra sum for the rubbish they bring down from the mountain.

## SIGHTSEEING

If you drive along the road from Ampenan to Senggigi, you will come across a
small Hindu temple, the ✹ *Pura Batu
Bolong (daily 7am–7pm)* on a rock above
the bay of the same name. The temple
is dedicated to Brahma, the god of creation, and there is an empty throne waiting for his arrival. The Hindus from western Lombok come here especially for the
full moon ceremonies. It is only a short
distance from here to the next rock, the
*Batu Layar,* with the tomb of the Muslim
saint Syeh Syayid Muhammad al Bagda-
di who is said to have brought Islam to
Lombok.

## FOOD & DRINK

Most of the restaurants provide a shuttle
service to and from the hotels outside of
town.

### ASMARA

Whether you choose Sasak specialities,
pasta or steak, this is one of the best
classic style restaurants in town; also
offering special meals for children and a
corner for them to play in. *Jl. Raya Seng-
gigi | tel. 0370 69 36 19 | Moderate*

### INSIDER TIP COCO BEACH ☺

There are a handful of *berugaks* (covered pavilions for sitting) around a
beach bar in the coconut grove north
of Senggigi where organic food from
their own garden and fresh drinks are
served. An ideal place to relax! *Pan-
tai Kerandangan | Pintu 2 | tel. 0817
5 78 00 55 | Budget*

### DE QUAKE

Sophisticated seafood creations and
cocktails are served in this simply decorated restaurant, which is located on

the beach behind the art market. *Art
Market | Jl. Raya Senggigi | tel. 0370
69 36 94 | Moderate*

### SQUARE

Probably the fanciest restaurant in
Senggigi, with one of the best chefs from
Bali. In the lounge on the first floor there
is club music in the evening. *Jl. Raya
Senggigi km 8 | tel. 0877 65 29 48 66 |
Expensive*

### TEMPTATIONS

Bakery and deli with the best selection
of western foods on Lombok. The café
serves a delicious breakfast and fresh
lunches. *Jl. Palm Raja 3 | Batu Bolong |
tel. 0370 69 34 63 | Moderate*

## SHOPPING

There are hawkers everywhere on the
beach during the day. Products from
all over Lombok can be found at the *art
market (pasar seni)* at the northern end
of town. The small shops in the centre of
Senggigi sell food, cosmetics and other
daily needs.

### ASMARA ART SHOP

The shop in front of the eponymous restaurant sells lovely fabrics and high-qual-
ity handicrafts. *Jl. Raya Senggigi | www.
asmara-group.com*

### AUTORE PEARL CULTURE

One of Lombok's largest pearl farms; all
of the pearls sold have a certificate of au-
thenticity. Tours are also organised. *Teluk
Nare | www.pearlautore.com*

## SPORTS & ACTIVITIES

Almost all of the diving organisations
have offices in Senggigi. Diving courses
can be booked from *Dream Divers (Jl.*

*Raya Senggigi kav. 15 | tel. 0370 69 37 38 | www.dreamdivers-lombok.com).*

The *Rinjani Trekking Club (Jl. Senggigi Raya, km 8 | Batu Layar | tel. 0370 69 32 02 | www.rinjanitrekclub.org)* can provide information for those who want to climb the Rinjani. *e-one Tours & Travel (Jl. Raya Senggigi (in front of the Asmara Artshop) | tel. 0370 69 38 43 | www.lomboktoursandtravel.com)* is a reliable vehicle rental company and also organises excursions.

Relax in the spas in the large hotels: the treatments in the S*heraton Senggigi Beach (Jl. Raya Senggigi | tel. 0370 69 33 33)* are especially recommended. Another place for very good – and much less expensive – massages is the simple *Lemongrass Spa (Jl. Raya Senggigi | tel. 0370 69 31 77).*

## BEACHES

Senggigi's main beach is full of small kiosks, hawkers and fishing and excursion boats. The Senggigi Beach Hotel rents deckchairs for 30,000 Rp – they are particularly popular at the sunset happy hour when there is also live music. The best place for swimming is at the beach in front of the Café Alberto in *Batu Bolong*. The beautiful beach at *Mangsit* has now been taken over by hotels but there are still peaceful stretches of beach lined with palm trees in *Klui, Malimba* and *Nipah* bays.

## WHERE TO STAY

### THE CHANDI

The boutique resort is located on the tranquil beach at Batu Layar. Restaurant, beach bar, pool and spa. *15 villas | Jl. Raya Senggigi | Batu Layar | tel. 0370 69 21 98 | www.the-chandi. com | Expensive*

### JEEVA KLUI

A spacious boutique hotel with a natural design has a chic restaurant and pool and is right on the tranquil beach at Klui. *35 suites | Jl. Raya Klui 1 | tel. 0821 50 00 08 00 | jeevaklui.com | Expensive*

### KILA SENGGIGI BEACH HOTEL

Lavish hotel complex on Senggigi's most central beach. Three restaurants, two bars, large pool and sports facilities. The hotel's exclusive *Pool Villa Club* has 16 two-storey villas with private Jacuzzi and pool access. *150 rooms | Jl. Pantai Senggigi | tel. 0370 69 32 10 | senggigi beachhotel.com | Moderate–Expensive*

### INSIDER TIP ▶ MAMA BELLA'S RETREAT

A tiny oasis in the middle of the village: Ten bungalows with slate roofs arranged around a lovely pool, very friendly service, 15 minutes from the beach. *Jl. Arjuna Tiga 11 | no tel. | mamabellaslombokretreat.com | Budget*

### INSIDER TIP ▶ THE PUNCAK ☼

Very friendly boutique hotel high up on 'The Hill', an exclusive villa district above Senggigi. Fabulous view. *5 rooms | The Hill | Batu Layar | tel. 0821 4710 45 37 | www.thepuncak.com | Moderate*

### QUNCI VILLAS

Stylish boutique hotel with three pools directly on the beach, spa. Two excellent restaurants serving Asian and Western fusion cuisine and a beach bar. *80 rooms | Jl. Raya Mangsit | tel. 0370 69 38 00 | www.quncivillas.com | Moderate–Expensive*

### SENDOK GUEST HOUSE

Charming budget hotel in the centre of town with a small pool and restaurant. *18 rooms | Jl. Raya Senggigi km 8 | tel. 0370 69 31 76 | www.sendokhotellombok. com | Budget*

## SUNSETHOUSE
Small, modern hotel right on the lovely beach at Batu Bolong; with pool and romantic Sunset Bar. *32 rooms | Jl. Raya Senggigi 66 | Batu Bolong | tel. 0370 692020 | www.sunsethouse-lombok.com | Budget–Moderate*

**WHERE TO GO**

### BANYUMULEK AND SUKARARA ★ ●
(140 B–C4) *(Ⴢ Q–R8)*
Around 24 km/14.9 mi from Senggigi is the pottery village of Banyumulek famous for its earthenware with simple designs. The pottery is now exported worldwide. In the morning, visitors can watch the potters firing their creations. The weaving centre Sukarara is about 15 km/9.3 mi further to the southeast. The women sit in front of their houses, with their legs stretched out in front of them, weaving at their looms. The elaborate fabrics are sold in the shop run by the village collective.

### GUNUNG PENGSONG ☼
(140 B4) *(Ⴢ Q8)*
An enchanted 16th century Hindu temple on a hill 27 km/16.8 mi from Senggigi that is populated by a band of cheeky monkeys. From here, you will have a wonderful panoramic view over West Lombok and – if the weather is fine – to the sea and the Rinjani. A buffalo is sacrificed here every year in March/April to invoke a good harvest. *Daily 7am–6pm | free admission | donations requested*

### TIU PUPUS AND KERTA GANGGA
(140 C2) *(Ⴢ R6)*
The 50 m/164 ft high *Tiu Pupus Waterfall* is 4.5 km/2.8 mi south of Gondang (around 30 km/18.6 mi north of Senggigi). Although there is not much water in the dry season, it is still worth making the pleasant walk. It is twice the distance to the impressive double-cascade waterfall, the *Air Terjun Kerta Gangga,* with a bathing pool and caves. Both waterfalls can also be reached by car.

Simple clay pots are made in the small potteries of Banyumulek

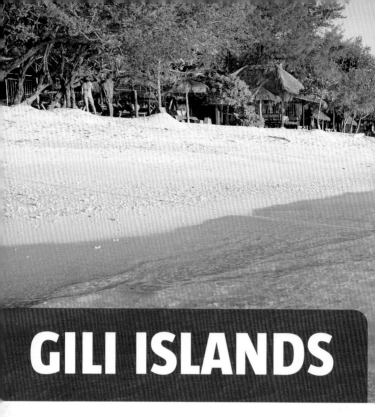

# GILI ISLANDS

**Strung like pearls in the glittering turquoise sea off the northwest coast of Lombok are Gili Air, Gili Meno and Gili Trawangan (simply called 'the Gilis') which just means 'small islands'.**

They are a heaven on earth for snorkellers, divers and holidaymakers who just want to relax on the beach. All of the three islands have crystal-clear waters surrounded by coral reefs, which you can access straight from the endless white ★ *beaches*. The view of the volcano Mount Rinjani from the eastern coasts is spectacular while in the evening everyone turns their gaze on Bali's Gunung Agung in the west. There are small bamboo pavilions *(berugak)* on the beaches where holidaymakers can relax and enjoy exotic drinks and snacks.

In the 1980s, the first backpackers discovered the largely uninhabited Gilis where previously only a few fishermen from northern Sulawesi had planted some groves of coconut palms. Bamboo huts and hammocks gave them a Robinson Crusoe atmosphere. Today, around 4000 people live on the car-free Gilis. The predominantly Muslim population is very tolerant, so you will have no trouble enjoying your holiday to the full – even during Ramadan – as long as certain fundamental rules (such as never sunbathing nude or topless) are observed.

Tourism only really took off in the last decade when the government initiated a campaign and massive investments came from abroad. Thanks to this it is possible to reach the Gilis directly from

**Coral reefs and bamboo bungalows in coconut groves form the perfect backdrop for a modern Robinson Crusoe holiday**

Bali. Since then, *Gili Trawangan* in particular has developed into a party island. An increasing number of cafés, bars and chic resorts are also opening their doors on *Gili Air* but there are still many idyllic retreats from all the hustle and bustle. *Gili Meno*, on the other hand, has managed to preserve its peaceful 'get away from it all' atmosphere. Horse-drawn carriages and bicycles are the only means of transport on all three islands.

However, you will have to hire a boat if you want to explore the really beautiful snorkelling and diving areas in the ★ *underwater world* off the Gilis because the corals close to the islands have been severely damaged by dynamite fishing. The Gili Eco Trust has been set up to attract to grow new corals on artificial reefs. Environmental awareness plays a major role on the small islands: for example, in order to avoid waste, the shops and cafés refill empty water bottles. Drinking water is scarce on the Gilis and the tap water is usually rather salty. There are also no uniformed policemen

An Eldorado for divers just a short boat trip away from the Gilis

on the islands – civil guards take care of security. There are now numerous ATMs on Gili Trawangan and you can get money from an ATM on Gili Air and Gili Meno. Credit cards are only accepted in the larger hotels and restaurants, as well as by most of the diving organisers. But as the transactions don't always work it is a good idea to take sufficient cash. Small clinics provide basic medical care but if you become seriously ill you should return to Lombok or Bali as soon as possible. There is mobile telephone reception and wi-fi on all three islands.

There are crossings from both Bali and Lombok *(speedboats from Benoa or Padang Bai | from 670,000 Rp, 1.5 hours | gili-fastboat.com; from Senggigi with Perama Tour | 150,000 Rp, 30 minutes | www.peramatour.com)*. There are public shuttles and private motor boats between the islands and *Bangsal*.

# GILI AIR

(143 D–F 4–6) *(Ⓜ s–u 4–6)* **Those who don't feel like partying but still want to have some company will feel at home on Gili Air – families in particular enjoy this island.**

Gili Air (which means 'water island') is the closest to Lombok and, with around 1500 inhabitants, more densely populated than the other Gilis. The island is covered in coconut groves and there are mainly simple bungalow resorts and beach cafés but an increasing number of restaurants and accommodations are opening. Most can be reached via the beach path that runs around the island. The best place for swimming and snorkelling is in the southeast. There are only limited shopping possibilities.

## FOOD & DRINK

**CHILL OUT BAR** (143 F6) *(⋒ u6)*
From breakfast with fresh juices to a seafood BBQ including cocktails – on the liveliest stretch of beach in the southeast. *Tel. 0370 62 03 70* | *Moderate*

**GILI AIR SANTAY** ⊘ (143 F5) *(⋒ u5)*
This is an institution on the island and famous for its Thai curries and shakes that are made exclusively with fresh, local products. One of the first restaurants with waste recycling. *In the northeast* | *tel. 0819 64 15 99 37 82* | *Budget*

**THE MEXICAN KITCHEN**
(143 E4) *(⋒ t4)*
Tacos, cocktails and salsa music are especially popular at the Sunset Happy Hour. Live music at the weekend. Bintang *Beach Tanjung* | *in the north-west* | *tel. 0878 64 12 22 00* | *Budget–Moderate*

**MOWIE'S BAR** ⋚ (143 E6) *(⋒ t6)*
Healthy sandwiches and power drinks, vegetarian dishes and raw food, plus first-class views of the sunset. *In the south-west* | *tel. 0878 64 23 13 84* | *Budget*

## SPORTS & ACTIVITIES

Most of the places offering accommodation also organise snorkelling and fishing excursions and rent the necessary equipment. Professional diving courses and tours are offered by: *Dream Divers (tel. 0370 63 45 47* | *dreamdivers.com* | (139 F6) *(⋒ u6))*, *Blue Marlin Dive (tel. 0370 63 99 80* | *www.bluemarlindive.com* | (139 F5) *(⋒ u6))* and the superb diving resort *Manta Dive (tel. 0813 37 78 90 47* | *www.manta-dive-giliair.com* | (139 F6) *(⋒ u6))*. In the centre of the island *H$_2$O Yoga (tel. 0877 61 03 88 36* | *www.h2oyoga andmeditation.com* | (139 E–F5) *(⋒ t–u5))*

organise yoga courses and meditation retreats, as well as good massages, in the east of the island.

## WHERE TO STAY

**BIBA BEACH VILLAGE** (143 F5) *(⋒ u5)*
Colourful bungalow complex with a good Italian restaurant directly on the east beach. *10 rooms* | *tel. 0819 17 27 46 48* | *Budget*

**DAMAI BUNGALOWS** (143 F5) *(⋒ u5)*
Four basic, clean bungalows with a pool and café in one of the best snorkelling areas in the quieter north-east. *Tel. 0370 37 36 96 15* | *damaibungalows.giliair@ gmail.com* | *Budget–Moderate*

**INSIDERTIP▶ MANUSIA DUNIA GREEN LODGE** ⊘ (143 E5) *(⋒ t5)*
Small eco resort with a lovely garden in the west. The charmingly furnished bungalows are made from natural materials. Terrific service. *6 rooms* | *Jl. Pantai Barat* | *tel. 0878 64 49 02 82* | *www.manusiadunia.com* | *Moderate*

---

★ **Beaches**
Relax in bamboo pavilions on the long white sandy beaches → p. 90

★ **Underwater world**
The corals, fish and sea turtles fascinate snorkellers and divers → p. 91

★ **Nightlife**
Whether in a cosy Irish pub or a cool lounge – party animals can celebrate all night on Trawangan → p. 95

**MARCO POLO HIGHLIGHTS**

**SENANG VILLA** (143 E6) (*ᗰ t6*)
Five modern bungalows around a pool, 50 m/164 ft from the south-west beach, which is especially popular at sunset. *Tel. 0878 64 85 67 86 | www.senang-villa. com | Moderate*

# GILI MENO

(143 D–F 1–3) (*ᗰ s–u 1–3*) **Gili Meno ('salt island') has a Robinson Crusoe feel: it is the smallest and most peaceful of the three Gilis.**
You can walk around the island, which got its name from the salt lake in the western part, in about ninety minutes. The loveliest spots for snorkelling are in the northwest, northeast and southeast of the island. On the main road in front of the Gazebo Hotel there is a *turtle station* that gives information about the endangered marine creatures.

## FOOD & DRINK

**INSIDER TIP ANA'S WARUNG**
(143 F1) (*ᗰ u1*)
Generous portions of good Indonesian cuisine served in one of the best spots

## LOW BUDGET

It is often cheaper to buy tickets for the speedboats to and from Bali directly from boat company than at travel agencies or representatives.

Instead of taking a charter boat between the islands, you can use one of the public shuttle boats – but be patient as the schedule is not always reliable.

for snorkelling. Fresh seafood BBQ in the evenings. *In the north-east | tel. 0878 61 69 63 15 | Moderate*

**DIANA CAFÉ** ☼ (143 D2) (*ᗰ s2*)
Shell-decorated beach berugaks (seat pavilions) with the best views of the sunset, complete with cold beer, barbecued fish and reggae. *In the west, directly above the salt lake | no tel. | Budget*

**MAHAMAYA BOUTIQUE RESORT RESTAURANT** ● ☼ ⊚ (143 D1) (*ᗰ s1*)
Chic beach restaurant at the eponymous boutique resort; enjoy fresh seafood, international and dishes made from organic ingredients. View of the setting sun. *North of the salt lake | tel. 0888 71 55 8 28 | Moderate*

## SPORTS & ACTIVITIES

The main attraction for snorkellers and divers is the *Gili Meno Wall*, with its rare corals, fish and sea turtles, in the northwest. All the diving centres on the Gilis offer tours to Gili Meno including *Blue Marlin Dive (tel. 0819 07 41 20 24 | www.bluemarlindive.com |* (139 F2–3) *(ᗰ u2–3))* and *Divine Divers (tel. 0852 40 57 07 77 | www.divinedivers.com |* (139 F2–3) *(ᗰ u2–3))* on the island itself. Most of the places providing accommodation also organise snorkelling excursions, and yoga courses can be booked through *Mao Meno (www.mao-meno. com |* (138 C4) *(ᗰ r4))*.

## WHERE TO STAY

**KEBUN KUPU KUPU ECO RESORT** ⊚
(143 E2) (*ᗰ t2*)
Stylish bungalow resort with a pool, garden and restaurant in a quiet location beside the salt lake. Sewage and solid waste management, solar power. *6 rooms |*

tel. 0878 65 73 24 31 | www.kupumeno resort.com | *Moderate*

**VILLA NAUTILUS** (143 F2–3) (*□ u2–3*)
Five comfortable stone bungalows with air conditioning, warm water, sundeck and beach café. *At the main beach in the southeast | tel. 0370 64 21 43 | www. villanautilus.com | Moderate*

INSIDER TIP **VILLA SAYANG**
(143 E1) (*□ t1*)
Two pleasantly decorated villas with separate living area, kitchen, open-air bath, and cleaning service in a spacious garden

**numerous hotels and restaurants in all price categories.**

Its reputation as a party island that is celebrated by some of the media as "Ibiza of the Far East" draws holidaymakers who are keen to enjoy Trawangan's spectacular ★ nightlife. As soon as the sunset cocktails are served most of the cafés and bars turn the music up full volume; afterwards you can chill out to lounge music, dance to oldies or rave to techno beats. But during the day, everything here revolves around the sea.

To keep misfortune far away from the Gilis, the *Mandi Sapa bathing ritual* is held

Unforgettable: the sunset at Gili Trawangan against the volcanic background

a little inland. Ideal for families. *North of the jetty | tel. 0818 36 10 52 | villasayang gilimeno.com | Moderate*

# GILI TRAWANGAN

(142 A–C 2–5) (*□ p–r 2–5*) **Gili Trawangan is the largest Gili and also the one most developed for tourism with**

on Trawangan every year at the end of the Islamic *Safar* month: hundreds of people carry offerings down to the sea and then they all go for a swim together. At the same time, newly hatched sea turtles are given their freedom. A local initiative has established a *turtle station (daily 8am–6pm | donations requested)* in the northeast of the island with the aim of protecting these endangered animals. For romantics: you will have the best view of sunrise and sunset in front of the volcanoes on Bali and Lombok from the ● top of the small hill in the south of the island.

## FOOD & DRINK

**KARMA KAYAK** (142 B2) (*∅ q2*)
Enjoy tapas and sangria as you watch the sun go down. *At the north beach | tel. 0818 05 59 37 10 | Budget*

**KAYU CAFÉ** (142 C4) (*∅ r4*)
Home-baked bread, freshly made sandwiches, cakes, crispy salads and healthy smoothies are served in this wooden vintage setting and on the beach terrace. *North of the harbour | tel. 0878 65 73 81 82 | Moderate*

**NIGHT MARKET (PASAR SENI)** (142 C4) (*∅ r4*)
Once the sun has set, locals and tourists alike enjoy tasting their way along the countless food stalls serving authentic Indonesian cuisine. *On the harbour | Budget*

**PEARL BEACH LOUNGE** (142 C5) (*∅ r5*)
Curvy bamboo architecture on the beach, the dishes on the menu ranging from Asian to American. *In the south-east | tel. 0813 37 15 69 99 | Expensive*

**INSIDER TIP THE YOGA PLACE GARDEN CAFÉ** ⊙ (142 B4) (*∅ q4*)
This basic organic café that serves delicious vegetarian dishes and fabulous juices is hidden on a hill behind the village. Also available: ● Yoga courses. *Jl. Ikan Pelatuk | tel. 0852 39 17 15 50 | Budget–Moderate*

## SHOPPING

In addition to your daily necessities, such as food, toiletries and postcards, it is also possible to buy local souvenirs and diving and snorkelling equipment here. More and more boutiques now also offer clothes and accessories. There is also an *art market (pasar seni)* held every evening at the harbour. Vendors sell cheap t-shirts, sarongs and handicrafts and there are local dishes on offer at the food stalls.

## SPORTS & ACTIVITIES

There are many diving and snorkelling spots around the island where you can see turtles, manta rays and sometimes even small sharks. Some small firms also organise diving courses and tours on Trawangan but the larger ones are more reliable: *Dream Divers (tel. 0370 6 13 44 96 | www.dreamdivers-lombok.com |* (142 C4) (*∅ r4*)), *Blue Marlin Dive (tel. 0370 6 13 24 24 | www.bluemarlindive. com |* (142 C4) (*∅ r4*)), *Manta Dive (tel. 0370 6 14 36 49 | www.manta-dive.com |* (142 C3) (*∅ r3*)).
The best angling spots for sports fishermen are in the northwest of the island. *Ko-Ko-Mo (tel. 0370 6 13 49 20 | kokomogilit@ ozemail.com.au |* (142 C4) (*∅ r4*)) is one of the companies that organise trips. If you don't want to walk around the island on foot (around 3 hours), you can hire a horse *(Stud Stables | tel. 0878 61 79 15 65 |* (142 B5) (*∅ q5*)). There are yoga classes every day at *Gili Yoga (tel. 0370 6 14 05 03 | www.giliyoga.com |* (142 C4) (*∅ r4*)).

## ENTERTAINMENT

The entire east coast of the island is full of places where you can go out and have fun. An official party plan lists those establishments where it is allowed to keep on rocking after 2am: Monday in the *Blue Marlin* (142 C4) (*∅ r4*), Wednesday in the *Tir Na Nog* (142 C5) (*∅ r5*) Irish Bar, Friday in *Rudy's Pub* (142 C4) (*∅ r4*) and Saturday in *Sama-Sama*

(142 C3) (*☐ r3*). However, parties are now held almost every night at several locations – and on a boat. The monthly *Fullmoon Rave* takes place on the southern beach. Ask your hotel about the special events.

## WHERE TO STAY

**DESA DUNIA BEDA** (142 B2) (*☐ q2*)
Tastefully furnished bungalows in the *Joglo* style (pyramid-like roof constructions), pool and a large garden, beach restaurant. *12 rooms | in the north-west | tel. 0370 6 14 15 75 | www.desaduniabeda. com | Moderate–Expensive*

**INSIDER TIP** **EXILE** ⊗
(142 A4) (*☐ p4*)
Simple, clean bamboo bungalows with open-air baths in the quiet southwest that deliver a real island feeling; romantic beach bar with sunset drumming, ecological water and waste management. *North of Sunset Point | tel. 0819 07 22 90 53 | lom bokhomes@gmail.com | Budget*

**GILI ECO BUNGALOWS** ⊗
(142 B2) (*☐ q2*)
Nine comfortable bungalows with open living rooms and private kitchens. Spacious garden, saltwater pool, restaurant and spa with organic products, coral project on the beach. *10 rooms | in the northwest | tel. 0361 8 47 64 19 | www. giliecovillas.com | Moderate*

**LUCE D'ALMA RESORT** ⊗
(142 B3) (*☐ q3*)
Modern luxury hotel with pool, spa and Italian restaurant, its own hydraulic system and solar power. *16 rooms | in the north, a little inland | tel. 0370 62 17 77 | lucedalmaresort.com | Expensive*

**PONDOK SANTI** ⊗
(142 A–B5) (*☐ p–q5*)
Ten lovely bungalows in a well cared for, spacious grove of coconut palms on the south beach; education and environment project right behind the complex. *Near Sunset Point | tel. 0370 6 14 51 86 | www.pondoksanti.com | Expensive*

If you don't want to walk, just take a seat on one of the horse-drawn carriages

# DISCOVERY TOURS

## ① BALI, LOMBOK AND THE GILI ISLANDS AT A GLANCE

**START:** ① Seminyak
**END:** ㉚ Kuta

10 days
Driving time
17 hours

Distance:
➡ 493 km // 306 mi

**COSTS:** 27,000,000 Rp for 2 people for transport, accommodation, meals, entrance charges

**WHAT TO PACK:** Fresh water, swimming things, sunscreen and insect protection, rain protection during the rainy season

**IMPORTANT TIPS:** ❼ **Ubud:** you need to be fit for the bike ride;
⑯ **Padang Bai:** book the crossing to the Gilis in advance;
⑰ **Gili Meno:** organise the evening excursion to ⑱ **Gili Trawangan** in advance through your accommodation

Would you like to explore the places that are unique to these islands? Then the Discovery Tours are just the thing for you – they include terrific tips for stops worth making, breathtaking places to visit, selected restaurants and fun activities. It's even easier with the Touring App: download the tour with map and route to your smartphone using the QR Code on pages 2/3 or from the website address in the footer below – and you'll never get lost again even when you're offline.

TOURING APP

→ p. 2/3

Experience the many facets of the islands: chic beach resorts and cultural centres on Bali, the tiny Gilis with their paradisiacal (underwater) world, and the picturesque bays and ancient traditions of Lombok.

The perfect place to arrive on **Bali** is ❶ **Seminyak** → p. 60. To speed up your recovery from your jetlag, stroll along the boutiques and cafés on **Jl. Kayu Aya** and enjoy your first sunset drink at the legendary beach club **Ku Dé Ta** → p. 63. As well as first-class music, it also has excellent food. You can catch up on your sleep at **Tony's Villas &**

DAY 1–2
❶ Seminyak

35 km / 21.8 mi

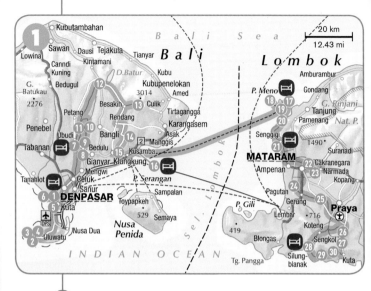

**2** Pura Luhur Uluwatu
🏯 🌴

2 km/1.2 mi

**3** Suluban
🏄 🏊 🌴

2 km/1.2 mi

**4** Padang-Padang
🏄 🏊 🌴

23 km/14.3 mi

**5** Kuta
🍺 🛍

9 km/5.6 mi

**6** Petitenget
🍸 🎵

DAY 3–4

36 km/22.4 mi

**7** Ubud
🏛 🏃 🍴 ⓘ 🎵 🚌

11 km/6.8 mi

**8** Goa Gajah
🚶 🏯

3 km/1.9 mi

Resort → p. 64, where you will spend two nights. On the second day, you'll take a moped trip to **Bukit Peninsula** → p. 37 and visit the **2** Pura Luhur Uluwatu temple → p. 37 in its spectacular cliff top location. **A narrow road** takes you from there to the bays **3** Suluban → p. 38 and **4** Padang-Padang → p. 38, where you can venture out onto a board yourself or watch the best surfers of the islands from the steep cliffs – and go for a dip, of course. On your way back, be sure to explore **5** Kuta → p. 44 with its numerous souvenir shops, and later on the club scene of **6** Petitenget.

Travel to **7** Ubud → p. 65, Bali's centre of culture and wellness, on the Perama shuttle bus → p. 124. After visiting the **Puri Lukisan** museum → p. 67, stroll to the 🌿 **Sari Organik** farm → p. 68 to sample the delicious organic dishes in the midst of the rice fields. There is **a circular trail** to the **Ubud Sari Health Resort** (*Jl. Kaleng 35 | tel. 0361 97 43 93 | www.ubudsari.com*), which offers massages in open garden pavilions. Feeling wonderfully relaxed, in the evening head for the **Puri Saren** → p. 68 to watch the dramatic *kecak* fire dance, then spend the first of two nights at the **Tjampuhan Hotel** → p. 72. Next day, borrow a mountain bike and cycle via the Elephant Cave **8** Goa Gajah → p. 72 to the anci-

# DISCOVERY TOURS

ent royal city of ⑨ **Pejeng → p. 73**, then on to ⑩ **Tampaksiring** and the mystical burial site of **Gunung Kawi → p. 73** and the holy springs of **Tirta Empul → p. 73**. Return **via the picturesque rice terraces** of ⑪ **Tegalalang** *(entrance 10,000 Rp.)*.

Hire a car and driver today. Your first destination is the lookout point ⑫ **Penelokan → p. 73**, which has numerous street cafés from where you have wonderful views of the active volcano Gunung Batur → p. 72. Take the **mountain roads** to ⑬ **Pura Besakih → p. 40** on the side of **Gunung Agung → p. 40**, Bali's highest volcano. **Winding roads flanked by lush vegetation take you to Sidemen**, where you can enjoy a rustic meal at the *warung* ⑭ **Ume Anyar** *(daily | tel. 0852 38 72 71 99 | Budget)* as well as the fabulous views of the deep green rice terraces. **Further south**, enjoy a stroll through ⑮ **Klungkung → p. 54** and see the old courthouse of **Kerta Gosa → p. 54**, which has some extremely impressive ceiling paintings. Then in the evening, relax by the pool, in the spa and in the restaurant of your accommodation, airy **Bloo Lagoon Village → p. 54** high above ⑯ **Padang Bai → p. 53**.

In the morning, arrange a ride to the **ferry harbour** and take a speedboat to ⑰ **Gili Meno → p. 94**. This is a wonderful place to relax, and especially at the **Villa Sayang → p. 95**, where you will spend two nights. Next day, hire a boat and snorkelling or diving equipment. The skippers know where to find the loveliest corals and where to see the sea turtles. Arrange to be dropped off at ⑱ **Gili Trawangan → p. 95** for the sunset, where you can enjoy the night life before taking a boat back to ⑲ **Gili Meno**.

Your next destination is **Lombok**. The speedboat stops at ⑳ **Teluk Nare**, where you will visit the **Autore** pearl farm → p. 87, and find out all about the cultivation of South Sea pearls. Then take a taxi **along the coastal route to** ㉑ **Senggigi → p. 86**. Enjoy the relaxed atmosphere in Lombok's tourist centre, and come sunset treat yourself to an evening meal and night at the elegant **Qunci Villas → p. 88**.

A car and chauffeur will take you on a journey of cultural discovery to the temple sites of ㉒ **Pura Lingsar → p. 81** and ㉓ **Taman Narmada → p. 82**. From

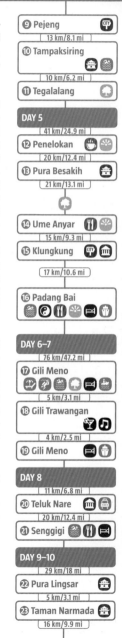

| ㉔ Banyumulek | 🛍 |
| --- | --- |
| 16 km/9.9 mi | |
| ㉕ Sukarara | 🛍 |
| 18 km/11.2 mi | |
| ㉖ Rambitan | 🍵 |
| 1 km/0.6 mi | |
| ㉗ Sade | 🍵 |
| 24 km/14.9 mi | |
| ㉘ Selong Belanak | 🏄 🏖 🍴 🛏 🚵 |
| 10 km/6.2 mi | |
| 🌳 | |
| ㉙ Mawun | 🏄 🏖 |
| 11 km/6.8 mi | |
| ㉚ Kuta | 🍵 🍴 |

there continue to the artisan villages of ㉔ **Banyumu-lek → p. 89** and ㉕ **Sukarara → p. 89**, where you can buy earthenware and woven fabrics at very good prices. Finally, visit the traditional Sasak villages of ㉖ **Rambitan → p. 79** and ㉗ **Sade → p. 79** and find out first-hand how simply the original native people of Lombok lived. From here, **continue north until the road turns to** ㉘ **Selong Belanak → p. 78 just past Sengkol**. On the wonderful beach, start looking forward to a delicious evening meal and two quiet nights at the **Sempiak Villas → p. 78**.

The best way to explore further hidden bays along the **coastal route** is by moped. In ㉙ **Mawun → p. 78**, stop for a last session riding the waves or for a swim before arriving at ㉚ **Kuta → p. 76**. After a stroll through the fishing village, end the tour at the **Ashtari** restaurant **→ p. 77**.

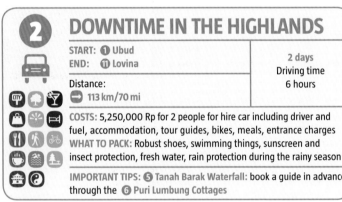

## **②** DOWNTIME IN THE HIGHLANDS

| START: **①** Ubud | |
| --- | --- |
| END: **⑪** Lovina | 2 days Driving time 6 hours |
| Distance: 🚗 113 km/70 mi | |

COSTS: 5,250,000 Rp for 2 people for hire car including driver and fuel, accommodation, tour guides, bikes, meals, entrance charges

WHAT TO PACK: Robust shoes, swimming things, sunscreen and insect protection, fresh water, rain protection during the rainy season

IMPORTANT TIPS: **⑤** Tanah Barak Waterfall: book a guide in advance through the **⑥** Puri Lumbung Cottages

Enjoy some peace yet experience a lot: in Bali's central Highlands you can enjoy the nature and be pampered in the spa, relax in hot springs and meditate in Bali's only Buddhist monastery.

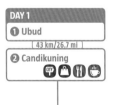

| **DAY 1** | |
| --- | --- |
| **①** Ubud | |
| 43 km/26.7 mi | |
| **②** Candikuning 🍵 🛍 🍴 ☕ | |

Your driver will arrive early for you in **①** Ubud **→ p. 65** and take you **along the main road to Bedugul, heading north** past rice fields and fruit plantations to **②** Candikuning **→ p. 49** at a height of approximately 1500 m/4921ft. This area is considered the agricultural heart of Bali, because fruit, vegetables and flowers flourish in its cool mountain climate. Take your time, and try the fresh fruit or spicy specialities on the **village market** (*daily*), because chilli, nutmeg and turmeric are also grown here. And when you feel

With a little luck, a dolphin will greet you at your destination Lovina

like a spot of breakfast, head for the original **INSIDER TIP**
**Eat Drink Love Coffee Shop** (*Budget*) in the middle of
the village square. **A little further down the road** is the
❸ **Pura Ulun Danu Bratan** → **p. 49** on a tiny island in
Lake Bratan. In clear weather, the eleven-step temple shrine and the impressive mountain backdrop are reflected in
the water. The Balinese come here to pray to the lake goddess for water for their fields.

**Drive north for a further 5 km/3.1 mi, then at Yehketipat
turn left to Danau Buyan and Danau Tamblingan → p. 49.
The narrow road runs high above the north shore,** which
is flanked by coffee and fruit plantations, along the shimmering turquoise waters of the lakes. The mountain slopes of the Gunung Batukaru → p. 64 rise up on the oppo-
site shore, while to the north the view reaches all the way
to the far-off sea.

In the village of **Munduk → p. 50**, fortify yourself with
a Balinese meal in the ❹ **restaurant** of the beautifully
situated **Puri Lumbung Cottages → p. 50**, where you will
also spend the night. From there, a guide will take you on

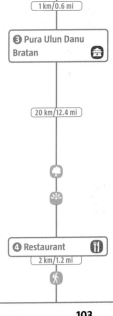

1 km/0.6 mi

❸ Pura Ulun Danu
Bratan

20 km/12.4 mi

❹ Restaurant

2 km/1.2 mi

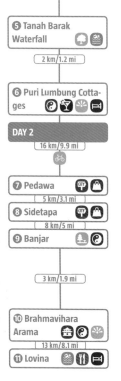

**⑤ Tanah Barak Waterfall** 🌳 🏞️

2 km/1.2 mi

**⑥ Puri Lumbung Cottages** ℹ️ 🍸 🌿 🛏️

**DAY 2**

16 km/9.9 mi

**⑦ Pedawa** 💬 🏠

5 km/3.1 mi

**⑧ Sidetapa** 💬 🏠

8 km/5 mi

**⑨ Banjar** 🏛️ ℹ️

3 km/1.9 mi

**⑩ Brahmavihara Arama** 🏛️ ℹ️ 🌿

13 km/8.1 mi

**⑪ Lovina** 🏖️ 🍴 🛏️

a hike through the coffee, vanilla, clove and avocado plantations to the **⑤ Tanah Barak Waterfall** *(daily 8am-4pm | admission 5000 Rp.)*. The water tumbles down into the natural pool from a height of 15 m/49.2 ft – wonderfully refreshing. On the way back from the hike, which takes about three hours, ask your guide how the rice is grown. Back at the **⑥ Puri Lumbung Cottages**, treat yourself to a Balinese massage and enjoy the views from the hotel's Sunset Bar.

Today, you and your local guide will cycle through traditional villages such as **⑦ Pedawa** and **⑧ Sidetapa**, where you can see how palm sugar is produced as well as various craft products made from bamboo. The four-hour tour **continues down** through deep-green rice terraces to the hot springs of **⑨ Banjar → p. 49**, where your driver will be waiting for you with your luggage. Settle down with your packed lunch that you have brought along from the hotel, if you haven't already done so, and relax in the sulphurous water (38 °C/100 °F) that bubbles up from the chiselled spouts and is said to have healing properties.

It's only another ten minutes to Bali's biggest Buddhist temple and only active Buddhist monastery **⑩ Brahmavihara Arama → p. 49**. You can meditate here, or simply enjoy the peace and the lovely views of the sea. It's only another 13 km/8.1 mi to your destination, **⑪ Lovina → p. 47**, with its black sand beaches. Highly recommended for dinner and accommodation is **The Damai → p. 48**.

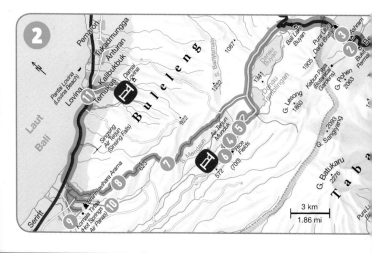

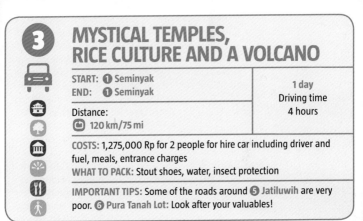

## 3 MYSTICAL TEMPLES, RICE CULTURE AND A VOLCANO

**START:** ❶ Seminyak
**END:** ❶ Seminyak

1 day
Driving time
4 hours

**Distance:**
🚗 120 km/75 mi

**COSTS:** 1,275,000 Rp for 2 people for hire car including driver and fuel, meals, entrance charges
**WHAT TO PACK:** Stout shoes, water, insect protection

**IMPORTANT TIPS:** Some of the roads around ❺ Jatiluwih are very poor. ❻ Pura Tanah Lot: Look after your valuables!

Explore three temples and learn about the ingenious system for cultivating rice on this day trip, the (literal) high point of which is on the island's second-highest volcano.

08:00am from ❶ Seminyak → p. 60 your driver will take you in your hire care to Mengwi → p. 65 and the ❷ Pura Taman Ayun → p. 65, which was founded in 1634. The royal temple at Mengwi is surrounded by a moat full of lotus flowers. It will have been worth the early start, because you can still enjoy the garden in peace before the travel groups descend on it.

❶ Seminyak
20 km/12.4 mi
❷ Pura Taman Ayun

8 km/5 mi

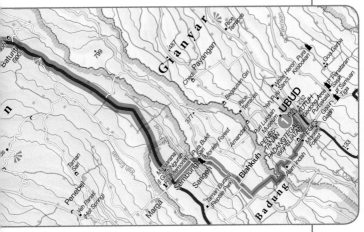

**③ Subak Museum** 🏛️

23 km/14.3 mi

Continue to Tabanan → **p. 65**, which is known as Bali's rice basket. Just before the little trade town is the small but highly interesting **③ INSIDER TIP Subak Museum** *(daily from 8am-5pm | admission 15,000 Rp.)*, which explains the cultivation of rice and the highly complex irrigation system. The *Subak* system, which is democratically based and based on egalitarian principles and the balance between the spiritual world, man and nature, is part of the Unesco World Heritage.

**From Tabanan there is a road north** to **Batukaru → p. 64**, Bali's second-highest volcano, which is covered in lush vegetation. Hidden in the jungle at a height of 825 m/2707 ft is the mystical temple **④ INSIDER TIP Pura Luhur Batukaru**, one of Bali's six holy temples. The shrines are dedicated to the mountain god and to the spirits of Lakes Bratan → p. 49, Buyan and Tamblingan → p. 49. The peace in this little-visited site contributes to its sacral mood, as do the swathes of mist that usually conceal the peak from view.

**12:00pm Travel back along the main road for about 2.5 km/1.6 mi to Wongayagede. There is a small winding road that goes east from here,** passing banana, chilli and coffee plantations to **⑤ Jatiluwih** *(access charge 25,000 Rp)*. On a clear day and in the cool mountain air, you will have fabulous views south, across the deep-green rice terraces, down to the sea. The centuries-old fields follow the natural lines of the mountain slopes, and present the Subak system in all its perfection. Enjoy a lunch break in the simple family **Warung Dhea Jatiluwih** *(Jl. Raya Jatiluwih | Moderate)* and try the red rice that is grown here, a product of the ⓒ *Jatiluwih Organic Red Rice Association of Farmers*, which preserves the traditional, pesticide-free cultivation of ancient rice varieties. Served with organic vegetables and fresh strawberry juice. In good weather, go for a walk through the fields.

**④ Pura Luhur Batukaru** 🏛️

9 km/5.6 mi

**⑤ Jatiluwih** 🌸 🌳 🍴 🚶

43 km/26.7 mi

**⑥ Pura Tanah Lot** 🏛️ 📷 🌸

17 km/10.6 mi

**① Seminyak**

# DISCOVERY TOURS

The drive continues through tiny mountain villages and past verdant rice terraces via **Angsri to Jl. Raya Senganan. There, you turn right heading south, then take the route via Penebel, which continues for about 25 km/15.5 mi to Tabanan, then travel for a further 18 km/ 11.2 mi** until you get to the legendary sea temple of ⑥ **Pura Tanah Lot → p. 65.** Baruna, the god of the sea, is honoured on a picturesque cliff just off the coast, while poisonous sea snakes watch over the shrine. Despite the mass of tourists, this temple is one of the loveliest places on Bali from which to watch the sun set.

**06:00pm** As soon as the glowing sun has disappeared in the sea, ask your driver to take you back to ① **Seminyak** via the **Tanah Lot Bypass**, which will take about 45 minutes.

Growing rice according to the Subak system is hard physical work

---

### ④ PANORAMIC TOUR OF NORTHERN LOMBOK

| START: ① Senggigi | 1 day |
| END: ① Senggigi | Driving time |
| Distance: ⊖ 190 km/118 mi | 4 hours |

**COSTS:** 1,500,000 Rp for 2 people for hire car including driver and fuel, meals, entrance charges
**WHAT TO PACK:** Swimming things, water, rain protection during the rainy season

**IMPORTANT TIPS:** ③ **Sidemen:** Better resist sampling the palm wine and palm "schnapps"; ④ **Pusuk Pass:** Only the intrepid should consider feeding the monkeys, and think of the leader first; ⑥ **Mosque:** You will need an interpreter, so book an English-speaking driver; ⑦ **Rinjani Mountain Garden:** Order lunch in advance

The tour is worth it just for the visit to the Sasak village of Segenter, but also takes you to other spectacular places in the north of Lombok.

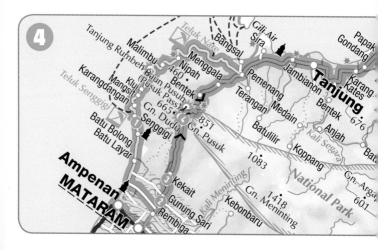

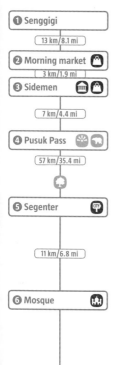

**1** Senggigi

*13 km/8.1 mi*

**2** Morning market 🛍️

*3 km/1.9 mi*

**3** Sidemen 🏛️🛍️

*7 km/4.4 mi*

**4** Pusuk Pass 🌸🐘

*57 km/35.4 mi*

🚻

**5** Segenter 💬

*11 km/6.8 mi*

**6** Mosque 🕌

**07:30am** Your hire car and driver will be waiting for you outside your hotel in **1** Senggigi → **p. 86** to take you to **Ampenan and then towards the Pusuk Pass. After branching off to Gunung Sari**, you will pass a **2** morning market where you can stock up on snacks. From here, continue towards **3** Sidemen. On the left side of the village street are a few palm sugar manufacturers. The farmers like to demonstrate how they make palm sugar, wine *(tuak)* and schnapps *(brem)* from the sap *(no set times)*. Fabulous views down to the sea await you at the top of the **4** Pusuk Pass and of the three islands off the coast – as well as hordes of nosy monkeys looking for treats. Continue through tiny towns and villages, past black sand beaches, until just before Sukadana **a road turns right to the traditional Sasak village** of **5** Segenter → **p. 85**. The people here live just as they did hundreds of years ago, in basic bamboo huts with dirt floors. A guide welcomes you at the entrance to the village to accompany you and tell you about the villagers' daily lives.

**Back on the main road**, continue to Bayan → **p. 84**, where you will find the oldest **6** mosque on Lombok, a simple construction of wood and bamboo. It is said that in 1634, one of the nine holy men who brought Islam to Indonesia founded the first Islamic community on Lombok. The residents of Bayan consider themselves to be his descendants, and follow the Wetu Teli faith which combines

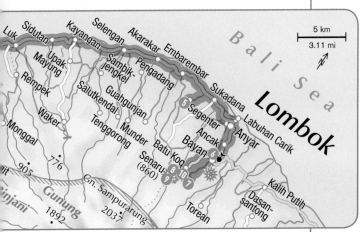

animistic and Hindu elements with Islam. As does the kee-
per of the shrine, who tells wonderful stories that your driver will translate for you. **The main road bears left past the
mosque, then continue straight on.**

`01:00pm` **Follow the track up the mountain for 3.7 km/
2.3 mi. Just after a left-hand bend turn hard right** into the
entrance of the ❼ **Rinjani Mountain Garden → p. 84**. The
owners have created a camping paradise with luscious
greenery and all sorts of animal inhabitants. Choose spicy
`INSIDER TIP` Sasak cuisine for lunch, and enjoy the views.
When you have cooled down in the pool, it's time to **return to Bayan and from there to the mountain village** of
❽ **Senaru → p. 83**, the starting point for trekking tours
to the volcano Gunung Rinjani → p. 85. You don't climb
up it however, but take the descent to the ❾ **Sindanggila Waterfall → p. 86**, which takes about 20 minutes,
and which thunders down powerfully in two steps from
50 m/164 ft into the valley. Right next to the entrance is
the ❿ **Pondok Senaru** (daily | tel. 0370 62 28 68 | Bud-
get), where you can enjoy a coffee with views of the waterfall on the way back.

`04:00pm` **Stay on the coastal road** for the drive back
to ❶ **Senggigi**. At sunset, a spectacular view of the Gili
Islands → p. 90 and Gunung Agung → p. 40 await you in
the bays to the **south of Bangsal**.

4 km/2.5 mi

❼ Rinjani
Mountain Garden

11 km/6.8 mi

❽ Senaru

1 km/0.6 mi

❾ Sindanggila
Waterfall

1 km/0.6 mi

❿ Pondok Senaru

82 km/51 mi

❶ Senggigi

# SPORTS & ACTIVITIES

**Whether in Bali, Lombok or the Gilis: you will have an enormous range of leisure activities.**

The focus is of course the sea with snorkelling, diving, sailing and surfing but there is also mountain biking, river rafting and – naturally – trekking tours to the volcanoes are very popular. Holidaymakers who are more interested in relaxation will find yoga classes, massages and spa treatments.

## DIVING & SNORKELLING

Among the most popular dive and snorkel spots on Bali are Pulau Menjangan and Nusa Penida, as well as the shipwrecks covered with corals off the eastern coast. The Gilis are a real paradise for snorkellers and divers. The gentle cur-

rents make the reefs there just perfect for beginners. One of Lombok's best diving areas is Sekotong Bay in the southwest of the island. On Bali, courses are offered by *Water Worx Dive Center (Padang Bai | tel. 0363 4 12 20| www.waterworxbali. com)* and *Eco Dive (Jemeluk | tel. 0363 2 34 82 | www.ecodivebali.com)*; on Lombok and the Gilis *Dream Divers (Senggigi/ Gili Trawangan/Gili Air | tel. 0370 69 37 38 | www.dreamdivers.com);* and *DSM Dive Lombok (Senggigi/Gili Trawangan | tel. 0370 69 32 80 | www.dsmlombok.com).*

## GOLF

The five golf courses on Bali and two on Lombok offer a superb selection. The *Bali National Golf Club* in Nusa Dua,

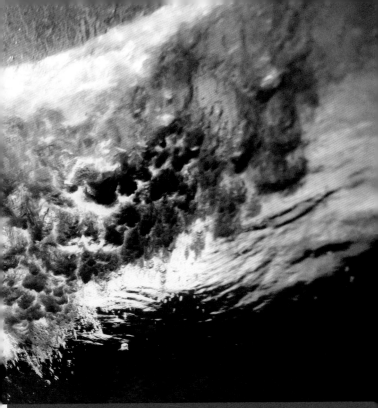

From the sea to the peaks: Bali, Lombok and the Gilis all offer a choice of activities and a variety of ways to relax

the *Bali Handara Kosaido Country Club* in the mountains, as well as the *Bali Nirwana Golf Club* near Tanah Lot, are among the best golf courses in Asia. The comparatively new ☆ *Lombok Golf Kosaido Country Club* has a wonderful location with views of the Gilis. With the exception of the nine-hole *Bali-beach Golf Course* in Sanur, all of the courses have eighteen holes. *Information and package deals under: www.bali.com/golf-courses.html or www.lombok-golf.com.*

## HIKING & TREKKING

The highlight for mountaineers is the hike (at least three days) up the *Gunung Rinjani* on Lombok. The *Gunung Agung* on Bali is also a challenge for many. The half-day tour on the *Gunung Batur* is less demanding but just as impressive. On no account set out on one of these tours without a guide! The tour organisers include *Bali Sunrise Trekking (tel. 0818 55 26 69 | www.balisunrisetours.com)* and *Rinjani*

National Park (Senaru/Mataram | tel. 0370 6 60 88 74 | www.rinjaninational park.com). The Swiss aid organisation ⊕ INSIDER TIP Zukunft für Kinder (Future for children) (tel. 0812 38 43 45 55 | www.zukunft-fuer-kinder.ch/en) organises exciting trekking tours in the north of the Gunung Batur to provide support for village projects there.

## HORSEBACK RIDING

Trotting through the villages and rice terraces in the hinterland, galloping along a beach or even going for a swim with the horses: there are many offers for horseback riding excursions like Island Horse Riding (tel. 0361 8 46 96 16 | www.baliislandhorse.com). Riding on Lombok is offered by Kuta Horses (tel. 0370 6 60 47 31 | www.horseridinglom bok.com), with treks through Sasak villages and the coastal landscape.

## MOUNTAIN BIKING

Bike tours are very popular in spite of the tropical climate. The surroundings of Ubud are particularly suitable for cycling: the roads there are more or less intact and not terribly busy. You can easily cycle to the excursion destinations around Senggigi via the back roads in the surrounding area. Trips to the eastern part of Lombok are more adventurous but also very beautiful. Tours in small groups, starting in Ubud, are organised by Bali Eco Cycling (tel. 0361 97 55 57 | baliecocycling.com) and Green Bike Tour (tel. 0361 8 69 96 92 | www.greenbiketour.com). INSIDER TIP Mountain Bike Lombok (tel. 0819 99 09 71 26 | www.mountainbikelombok. com) in Senggigi not only offers day trips but also interesting multiday tours.

## RIVER RAFTING

The most popular is the roughly two-hour white water trip in an inflatable raft through the gorges of the Ayung River near Ubud. The tour on the Telaga Waja River on the Gunung Agung is more demanding – and you can be sure that your clothes will get wet! All of the organisers collect their guests from their hotels, such as Bali Adventure Rafting (Ubud | tel. 0361 72 14 80 | www.baliadventurerafting. com) and Sobek Bali Utama (Ubud/Kuta | tel. 0361 72 90 16 | www.balisobek.com).

## SAILING

From a modern ocean-going catamaran to a traditional Bugis schooner: numerous operators offer a variety of sailing trips. Most cruises last from one day to a week and nearly all depart from Bali for the east. Nusa Lembongan is just one of the destinations of day trips; longer cruises also take in Lombok, Komodo and Flores such as with Adelaar Cruises (tel. 0812 3 80 27 41 | www.adelaar-cruises.com and Sea Trek (Sanur | tel. 0361 27 06 04 | www. seatrekbali.com). You can find more cruise offers under: www.balicruises.com. Some hotels, such as the Grand Hyatt in Sanur and the Four Seasons in Jimbaran, have Laser or Hobie cats available for hire for guests wanting smaller sailing adventures.

## SPA TREATMENTS

Whether traditional Balinese massage, shiatsu or reflexology: at least one day of any holiday on Bali should be devoted to spa treatments. A massage on the beach lasting around one hour costs about 50,000 Rp – but it is worth spending more to be treated by trained masseurs in a spa and then relax in a whirlpool bath. There are spas on every corner and in almost all the hotels on Bali; on Lombok, mainly in the larger establishments. You can find a selection of recommended spas at: *www.balispaguide.com*.

## SURFING

Bali and Lombok are dream destinations for surfers. The surf rolls steadily on to the beaches from Kuta to Canggu – making them ideal for beginners. The huge waves at the southwest tip of Bali – for example at Padang-Padang, Bingin and Uluwatu – are best left to the experts! The beaches in southern Lombok are still considered an insider tip; especially Mawi, Gerupuk and – for real experts – Desert Point on the southwest tip of the island. Surfing courses, board rentals and organised tours on Bali can be booked from the *Bali Green Surf School (Seminyak | tel. 0819 99 34 41 22 | www. baligreensurf.net)* or *Padang Padang Surf Camp (Pecatu | Bukit Badung | tel. 0819 99 28 35 49 | www.balisurfingcamp.com)*, and from *Lombok School of Surf (Jl. Raya Pantai Kuta | tel. 0812 39 32 19 15 | www. lombokschoolsurfing.com)* on Lombok.

## YOGA

Bali has developed into a centre of yoga over the past decade: yoga classes are included by many hotels, such as *Desa Seni (www.desaseni.com)* in Canggu and *Zen Resort (www.zenresortbali.com)* near Lovina. The *Bali Spirit Festival (www.balispirit festival.com)* is held in Ubud every year in March/April and attracts participants from all over the world. The yoga wave has also arrived on Lombok and the Gilis. Yoga courses are offered e.g. in Kuta by *Ashtari (www.facebook.com/AshtariYoga)*, on Gili Air by *H2O Yoga (www.h2oyogaandmedi tation.com)* and on Gili Trawangan by *The Yoga Place (www.theyogaplacegili.com)*.

You don't have to climb a volcano: there are lots of lovely hiking paths on Bali

# TRAVEL WITH KIDS

Bali in particular is a good holiday destination for children. The well-developed beaches and the exotic culture provide plenty of fun and entertainment: they can snorkel, the first attempts at surfing or experience the exotic nature up close. And even little ones can go on courses to learn Balinese dancing or gamelan, how to make an offering or arts and crafts. Lombok and the Gilis are ideal for active holidays with older children – as well as water sports, there are also easy hiking and cycling tours. As a precaution, you should make sure that you have medication for diarrhoea, fever and colds, as well as a disinfectant. In the tropics, even small wounds can quickly become infected and should be cleaned immediately. The strong sun means that children should always have sunblock on, wear a hat and drink a lot of liquids. You should also regularly apply mosquito repellent to avoid Dengue fever and malaria (particularly on Lombok and the Gilis) and sleep under a mosquito net. Arms, legs and feet should always be covered at dusk. The best places on Bali for spending a holiday with children are *Amed, Nusa Dua, Sanur* and *Ubud. Gili Air* is also very popular

with families. Further information can found under: *www.baliwithkids.com, www.littlebalilove.com* and *www.bali forfamilies.com.*

## BALI TREETOP ADVENTURE PARK
(135 E4) (*ij J3*)
You would like to swing through the trees like monkeys? Well, you can in this lovely climbing park with seven levels of difficulty so everyone, from toddlers to adrenalin junkies, will find what they want. All the rope trails comply with European standards. *Daily 8.30am–6pm | Admission 25 US$, children to age 12 16 US$ | Eka Karya Botanical Garden | Candikuning | tel. 0361 9 34 00 09 | www. balitreetop.com*

## BUBBLEMAKER COURSES
Many providers organise snorkelling and diving courses for children. From the age of eight in a pool and in the open sea for those over ten. Starting from 970,000 Rp, *Crystal Divers (Jl. Danau Tamblingan 168 | Sanur | tel. 0361 28 67 37 | www.crystal-divers. com | (139 D4) (ij K7))* or *Ok Divers (Jl. Silayukti | Padang Bai | tel. 0811 3 85 88 25 | www.okdiversbali.com | (136 C6) (ij M5))* offer diving courses.

Climbing in the rainforest, riding elephants, exploring the underwater world – there are plenty of exciting experiences for children

### DISCOVER THE RAINFOREST ✪
(135 D5) (*ω H4*)

The INSIDER TIP *Sarinbuana Eco-Lodge* (p. 65) organises excursions for families to plantations and into the rainforest: everybody will learn a great deal about exotic animals and plants and also discover natural bathing spots and idyllic temples. Children can also help with feeding the numerous animals, learn how to make offerings or dress up as Balinese. The little ones also join in with picking and cooking. *Price from 200,000 Rp, free for children under the age of 15 | Mount Batukaru | Tabanan | www.baliecolodge.com*

### TEMPLE DANCE AND HANDICRAFTS

Most children are fascinated by Balinese musical instruments, dances and temple festivals and would love to take part in them. Particularly in Ubud (139 D2) (*ω J–K5*), many introductory courses are offered where children can learn the basics of gamelan music and simple dance steps, as well as making batiks, carving or preparing temple offerings. The *ARMA Museum (520,000 Rp | Jl. Raya Pengosekan | Ubud | tel. 0361 97 57 42 | www.armabali.com)* and the dance and music workshops of the INSIDER TIP *Mekar Bhuana Conservatory (from 39 US$ | Jl. Gandapura III/501x | Banjar Kesiman Kertalangu | Denpasar* (139 D4) (*ω J6*) *| tel. 0361 46 42 01 | www.balimusicanddance.com)* are especially recommended for their courses for kids.

### WATERBOM PARK (139 C5) (*ω H7*)

Fun for all the family is guaranteed in area covering over 9 acres. There are suitable entertainments for each age group, as well as a spacious pool complex and spa, and bars and cafés. *Daily 9am–6pm | 520,000 Rp, children to the age of 12 370,000 Rp | families (2 adults, 2 children) 1,630,000 Rp | Jl. Kartika Plaza | Kuta | www.waterbom-bali.com*

# FESTIVALS & EVENTS

No matter whether it is the Balinese New Year, the Islamic Feast of the Sacrifice or Christmas that is being celebrated, in Indonesia the major festivals of all the religions are public holidays.

## MUSLIM HOLIDAYS

The *Muslim holidays* vary according to the Islamic lunar calendar. Ramadan ends with the *Idul Fitri (Lebaran)*, the most important Muslim festival in Indonesia (2018: 15./16.6., 2019: 4./5.6., 2020: 24./25.5.). Prayer sessions and torchlight processions are held on the night before the celebrations. All Indonesians have holidays and flights and hotels are often fully booked. Other holidays are: Islamic New Year, *Maulid Nabi* (Birthday of the Prophet), *Isra Mi'raj* (Night Journey and Ascension of the Prophet), *Idul Adha* (Islamic Feast of the Sacrifice).

## BALINESE HOLIDAYS

Temple festivals on Bali are colourful events with processions, prayers, dancing and music. They are determined by the *Wuku* calendar that only has 210 days.
★ ● *Galungan/Kuningan* is the highlight of the Balinese year (2018: 30.5.–9.6.

and 26.12.–5.1., 2019: 24.7.–3.8., 2020: 19.–29.2. and 16.–26.9.). Ritual meals are prepared for the celebration that lasts ten days and there is dancing, music, shadow puppet theatre and processions.

Drums, gongs and rattles drive out the evil spirits on the night before the New Year's festival *Nyepi*. The following day is one of fasting and meditation. Nobody is allowed to leave the house; traffic comes to a standstill – and there are also no flights! ● *Odalan* is the anniversary of a temple. During the day, the ancestors are revered with prayers and offerings, and there are performances in the evening. The many temples mean that there is always an Odalan festival taking place. During the *Usaba Sambah Festival,* young men fight using thorny Pandanus leaves as weapons.

## SASAK FESTIVALS

At full moon in February/March, the Sasak gather on the beaches in the south of Lombok to catch Nyale worms between the corals to celebrate *Bau Nyale*. This fertility ritual is something of a marriage market for young people.
The ● *Perang Topat* ('Rice Cake War') takes place at the beginning of the rainy

season (usually in December) in the Pura Lingsar temple complex. Sasak and Hindus pelt each other with rice wrapped in palm leaves that is then buried to ensure a good harvest.

*Perisean* fights are held in Mataram and Narmada in August. Opponents battle each other with rattan sticks and bamboo shields; the first one to shed some blood, loses.

## OTHER EVENTS

### MARCH/APRIL
Yoga and meditation fans get together for the *Bali Spirit Festival* in Ubud.

### MAY
INSIDER TIP ▶ *Ubud Food Festival:* with Indonesia's top chefs

### JUNE/JULY
*Bali Art Festival:* for one month, Bali's best artists show their skills in Denpasar. *www.baliartfestival.com*

### AUGUST TO NOVEMBER
Speed, attitude and racing style are the main criteria in the *water buffalo races* in Jembrana in western Bali.

### OCTOBER
*Ubud Writers & Readers Festival:* authors have selected this as one of the most pleasant literature festivals. *www.ubudwritersfestival.com*

## PUBLIC HOLIDAYS

| | |
|---|---|
| 1 Jan. | Christian New Year |
| Jan./Feb. | *Imlek* (Chinese New Year) |
| March/April | *Nyepi* (Balinese New Year), Good Friday, *Isra M'raj* (Mohammed's Night Journey and Ascension) |
| 1 May | Labour Day |
| 1 June | *Pancasila* |
| May/June | *Idul Fitri* (end of Ramadan), Ascension Day, *Waisak* (Buddhist New Year) |
| Aug./Sept. | *Idul Adha* (Muslim Day of Sacrifice), Muslim New Year |
| 17 Aug. | Independence Day |
| Nov./Dec. | *Maulid Nabi* (Mohammed's Birthday) |
| 25 Dec. | Christmas day |
| Various months | *Galungan/Kuningan* (Temple Festival, see p. 116 for dates) |

# LINKS, BLOGS, APPS & MORE

www.bali.com Everything you need to know about your destination at a glance: accommodation links, community culture, ecotourism and offers ...

beatmag.com/bali The hippest nightclubs, the trendiest organic menus and a lot of news about international celebrities on Bali can be found in the online ekly entertainment guide

www.jed.or.id The network for ecological village tourism offers holidays with local families in four traditional villages on Bali

http://indonesia.travel/en/destination/73/bali History, sightseeing, spas, flora and fauna – the official tourism website has many tips to help you plan your Bali holiday

giliecotrust.com The environmental protection organisation's beach cleaning, coral and sea turtle projects all need volunteers to support their efforts, see their website for details about how you can get involved

short.travel/bal1 Professional blog with fabulous photos, videos and lots of information on the less frequented parts of the islands

www.thebalibible.com Travel features and plenty of best-of lists by locals, tourists and Bali lovers

janetdeneefe.com Restaurant owner Janet de Neefe not only founded the Ubud Writers & Readers Festival but also writes cookbooks and columns on Balinese cuisine that reveal a great deal about the cultural life of the island

www.pedulianak.org Two Dutchmen founded the Indonesian aid organisation that provides Lombok's street children with a home, an education and healthcare

Regardless of whether you are still preparing your trip or already in Bali: these addresses will provide you with more information, videos and networks to make your holiday even more enjoyable

www.thebalitimes.com Daily online English newspaper with local and international events, travel info and more

www.youtube.com/watch?v=SwLjkMCbgkk a slideshow entitled 'Best of Bali' as part of the GeoBeats travel series

short.travel/bal2 Music video by the very popular Indonesian band Navicula about Nyepi (Hindu New Year): „Saat semua semakin cepat, Bali berani berhenti". (When everything else speeds up, Bali dares to stop)

**VIDEOS & MUSIC**

short.travel/bal3 The eight-minute film shows the fascinating underwater world of the Gilis

short.travel/bal4 Short film about the Green School of Bali and the ideas of its founder John Hardy, which greatly influenced the island's education system, ecological awareness and architecture

short.travel/bal5 Impressive scene of a *kecak* dance in Gunung Kawi, taken from the documentary film „Baraka" by Ron Fricke (1992)

Bali Map A free navigational app that has information about the main sights, cafés, hotels and other useful addresses

**APPS**

Lombok Guide Offline maps, information on transport, accommodation and sights – free

Bali Kids This is a helpful app for parents with tips about family-friendly hotels and activities for children

Go-Jek App, which follows the Uber model and can be used to book (motorbike) taxis, food delivery services, boat trips and much more, anywhere in Indonesia

Waze This app continues to work when Google Maps starts to struggle: it includes hidden streets and knows about tiny restaurants, and also provides the latest traffic news so you can find the correct and fastest routes

# TRAVEL TIPS

## ARRIVAL

The Ngurah Rai international airport near Denpasar is served by many international airlines, usually with a stopover in Singapore or Kuala Lumpur. There are also flights to Lombok from both cities: *Silk Air (www.silkair.com)* from Singapore, *Air Asia (www.airasia.com)* and Garuda Indonesia *(www.garuda-indonesia.com)* from Kuala Lumpur. The flight from Europe takes between 14 and 20 hours depending on the route and number of stopovers on the way. The flight from Denpasar to Lombok takes around 25 minutes: *Garuda Indonesia, Lion Air and Wings Air (for both visit: www.lionair.co.id)* and *Merpati (www.merpati.co.id)* have daily flights. Several airlines fly from Jakarta to Bali and Lombok – the cheapest is *Air Asia (www.airasia.com)*.

Ferries run constantly between all the Indonesian islands. The 4½ hours crossing from Padang Bai (Bali) to Labuhan Lembar in the south-west of Lombok costs about 45,000 Rp. There are also speedboats from Benoa or Padang Bai to the Gilis and to Senggigi (from about 450,000 Rp), with a stop in Teluk Nare in the northwest of Lombok *(various providers | gili-fastboat.com or gilifastboats.com)*.

There are several buses every day from Jakarta to Denpasar *(around 1200 km/745 mi | travel time 24 hours/from 450,000 Rp)* that make the crossing to Bali on the car ferry. The bus trip from Denpasar to Mataram takes about seven hours.

## CAR HIRE

It is possible to rent mopeds and cars everywhere on Bali, as well as in Senggigi (Lombok); an international driving license is all that is necessary and the rates are very reasonable. Rental companies usually only offer their cars to drivers who are older than 21. A car with a driver who knows his way around (700,000 Rp/day) makes travelling much more pleasant. Take note: moped riders have to wear a helmet!

## CONSULATES & EMBASSIES

### USA CONSULAR AGENCY
*Jl. Hayam Wuruk 310 | Denpasar 80235 | Bali | tel. 0361 23 36 05 | after hour emergencies: 0361 24 68 59 | Mon–Fri 9am–3.30pm*

### BRITISH CONSULATE
*Jl. Tirta Nadi 2 No. 20| Sanur | Bali |*

## RESPONSIBLE TRAVEL

It doesn't take a lot to be environmentally friendly whilst travelling. Don't just think about your carbon footprint whilst flying to and from your holiday destination but also about how you can protect nature and culture abroad.

As a tourist it is especially important to respect nature, look out for local products, cycle instead of driving, save water and much more. If you would like to find out more about eco-tourism please visit: *www.ecotourism.org*

# From arrival to weather

**Holiday from start to finish: the most important addresses and information for your trip to Bali, Lombok and the Gili Islands**

*tel. 021 23 56 52 00 | Mon, Wed, Fri 8.30am–noon*

## CUSTOMS

Each person may bring 1 litre of spirits, 200 cigarettes or 100g of tobacco, into Indonesia. It is prohibited to bring firearms and pornographic material into the country, drug smuggling carries the death penalty. Electronic appliances must be taken out of Indonesia on departure. Export permission is required for antiques more than 50 years old and it is prohibited to export protected animals and plants (including corals!).

Travellers to the US who are residents of the country do not have to pay duty on articles purchased overseas up to the value of 800 US$, but there are limits on the amount of alcoholic beverages and tobacco products. For the regulations for international travel for US residents please see *www.cbp.gov*

## DRIVING

In Indonesia traffic drives on the left. Traffic on Bali and Lombok is chaotic and the roads are not especially good – particularly in the rainy season. The Gilis Islands are car-free areas. If you decide to risk getting behind the wheel on your holiday, you should bear the following in mind: the person who has right of way, is the one who takes it. If somebody toots his horn, he wants to pass; if he flashes his lights, it means 'I come first'. Waving with the fingertips pointing down and the back of the hand to the front means 'come here'. Self-proclaimed 'parking attendants' usually help you in your efforts to get into or out of a parking space – for a few rupiahs.

## ELECTRICITY

The voltage is 220 Volt. Plug sockets are the two-pin variety; adapters are inexpensive and available everywhere.

## BUDGETING

| | |
|---|---|
| Coffee | 1.25 £/1.60 $ *for a cup* |
| Nasi Goreng | 2.20 £/2.90 $ *for a serving* |
| Petrol | 0.40 £/0.52 $ *for a litre* |
| Car with driver | 40 £/52 $ *hire charge per day* |
| Diving course | 57 £/75 $ *for an introductory course* |
| Massage | 9 £/11.50 $ *for one hour* |

## EMERGENCY NUMBERS

Ambulance: *tel. 118*
Fire brigade: *tel. 113*
Police: *tel. 110*, police station in Kuta (Bali): *tel. 0361 75 15 98*, police station in Mataram (Lombok): *tel. 0370 62 11 24*

## HEALTH

It is recommend to be vaccinated against diphtheria, hepatitis A, polio, tetanus and typhoid. You should also have anti-malaria medication with you – especially if you are planning to visit Lombok and the Gilis. In addition, it is advisable to take out a health insurance that includes repatriation costs. Avoid drinking tap water and only eat ice cream and fruit in the better restaurants.

Many of the large hotels on Bali have a doctor in the house. The following clinics on Bali can be recommended for tourists: *BIMC Hospital Bali (Jl. Bypass Ngurah Rai No. 100X | Kuta | tel. 0361 76 12 63 | www. bimcbali.com)* and *International SOS Medical Clinic (Jl. Bypass Ngurah Rai 505X | Kuta | tel. 0361 71 05 05 | www.sos-bali.*

A moped may also be used to transport reeds

*com).* The best clinic on Lombok is the *Harapan Keluarga International Hospital (Jl. Ahmad Yani 9 | Selagalas | Mataram | tel. 0370 6 17 70 20 | harapankeluarga. co.id).* If you fall seriously ill, it is best to fly out to Singapore. Medicines can be purchased in pharmacies *(apotik)* and drugstores (*toko obat*).

## IMMIGRATION

There are two kinds of visas for entry into Indonesia, certain passport holders must apply for a 'Visa in Advance' while others are eligible for the 'Visa on Arrival' option. In order to find out which is applicable you will need to contact your travel agent or an Indonesian embassy. Either way your passport must be valid for at least six months from date of arrival in the country. You fill out an arrival card on the plane and retain your departure card in your passport until you leave the country. A tourist visa can be extended once for 30 days.

## INFORMATION

**EMBASSY OF INDONESIA USA** – *2020 Massachusetts Ave NW | Washington DC 20036 | tel. 202 775 52 00 | www.embassy ofindonesia.org*

**EMBASSY OF INDONESIA UK** – *Visa and Consular Section | 38A Adams Row | London W1K | tel. 020 74 99 76 61 | www. indonesianembassy.org.uk*

**BALI TOURISM BOARD**
*Jl. Raya Puputan 41 | Renon | Denpasar | Bali 80235 | tel. 0361 23 56 00 | www. balitourismboard.org*

## INTERNET CAFÉS & WI-FI

Most of the hotels and restaurants on Bali, Lombok and the Gilis provide free Wi-Fi access; however, the connection is often poor in the more remote areas. There are only few internet cafés left. USB modems for laptops can be bought from Smartfren, Telkomsel or XL *(2 GB/30 days from 50,000 Rp)* and other providers.

## MONEY & CURRENCY EXCHANGE

The Indonesian currency is the Indonesian rupiah (Rp). There are 50, 100, 200,

500 and 1000 Rp coins, as well as 1000, 2000, 5000, 10,000, 20,000, 50,000 and 100,000 Rp notes. Many hotels calculate their prices in US$ or euros to compensate for the great fluctuation in the exchange rates, but usually you have to pay in rupiah.

Banks are open from Mon–Thu from 8.30am–2pm, Fri 8.30am–11.30am. Moneychangers do business from 8am–8pm and often offer better rates than the banks (beware of cheats and always check the official rates!). There are cash dispensers (ATMs) almost everywhere where you can withdraw money using your EC or credit card and PIN code. Most hotels and shops also accept credit cards.

## OPENING HOURS

There are no set opening times in Indonesia. While markets and food shops get busy from sunrise, boutiques and other shops might not open until midday. But most will then remain open until late at night, especially in tourist areas. This also applies on Sundays and public holidays, with the exception of *Nyepi*, where everything on Bali is closed. Lots of shops and restaurants on Bali are also closed on *Galungan* and *Kuningan*. On Lombok this applies on *Idul Fitri*, especially in more remote areas.

## PERSONAL SAFETY

The most dangerous thing on Bali and Lombok is the traffic. You can feel safe wherever you go, even after dark. However, women travelling alone should be prepared for verbal flirting. Petty crime is mainly in the tourist resorts, usually by motorcyclists, who grab bags as they ride past. So it is a good idea to only have things you need with you including a copy of your passport and visa. Credit

cards etc. are best kept in the hotel safe. Do not leave any valuables unattended on the beach or in your car!

## PHONE & MOBILE PHONE

To call home from Bali dial 001 then your country code (UK 44; USA and Canada 1). Telephone calls are cheaper if you dial 007 before the country code

## CURRENCY CONVERTER

| £ | IDR | IDR | £ |
|---|---|---|---|
| 1 | 17,000 | 1000 | 0.06 |
| 3 | 51,000 | 5000 | 0.30 |
| 5 | 85,000 | 12,000 | 0.72 |
| 13 | 221,000 | 30,000 | 1.80 |
| 40 | 680,000 | 80,000 | 4.80 |
| 75 | 1,275,000 | 150,000 | 9 |
| 120 | 2,040,000 | 240,000 | 14.40 |
| 200 | 3,400,000 | 600,000 | 36 |
| 500 | 8,500,000 | 1,000,000 | 60 |

| $ | IDR | IDR | $ |
|---|---|---|---|
| 1 | 13,500 | 1000 | 0.08 |
| 3 | 40,500 | 5000 | 0.40 |
| 5 | 67,500 | 12,000 | 0.96 |
| 13 | 175,500 | 30,000 | 2.40 |
| 40 | 540,000 | 80,000 | 6.40 |
| 75 | 1,012,500 | 150,000 | 12 |
| 120 | 1,620,000 | 240,000 | 19.20 |
| 200 | 2,700,000 | 600,000 | 48 |
| 500 | 6,750,000 | 1,000,000 | 80 |

For current exchange rates see www.xe.com

when using the fixed-line network. If you do not have a telephone in your hotel, you can go to a *wartel* (telephone shop). The dialling code for Indonesia is 0062. Bali has the following area codes: (0)361 in the south, (0)362 in the north, (0)363 in the east, (0)365 in the west and (0)366 for Klungkung. Lombok and the Gilis can be reached under (0)370. You can make economical mobile telephone calls or you can message with an Indonesian prepaid card that can be recharged on every street corner.

## PHOTOGRAPHY

As a rule, the local population has no objections to being photographed or filmed but you should still ask for permission beforehand. You should show particular restraint in temples and mosques; always ask for permission and never focus directly on the face of a priest. An extra fee is often charged for using a camera at special places of interest.

## POST

Each major town has a post office *(kantor pos, Mon–Thu 7.30am–3pm, Fri 7.30am–11.30am, Sat 7.30am–1pm)*. It is also often possible to hand in your post at your hotel. Airmail *(pos udara)* takes one to two weeks to reach Europe. A postcard costs 7500 Rp, a standard letter 15,000 Rp.

## PUBLIC TRANSPORT

Drivers offer their services on every street corner; the price is always subject to your negotiation skills. Hotels can also organise transport but they often charge for this service. Private shuttle buses, such as those operated by *Kura Kura Bus (www.krua2bus.com)* or *Perama Tours*

# WEATHER IN DENPASAR

| | Jan | Feb | March | April | May | June | July | Aug | Sept | Oct | Nov | Dec |
|---|---|---|---|---|---|---|---|---|---|---|---|---|
| Daytime temperatures in °C/°F | 30/86 | 30/86 | 30/86 | 31/88 | 31/88 | 30/86 | 30/86 | 31/88 | 31/88 | 32/90 | 32/90 | 30/86 |

| Nighttime temperatures in °C/°F | 22/71 | 23/73 | 23/73 | 23/73 | 23/73 | 23/73 | 22/71 | 22/71 | 22/71 | 23/73 | 23/73 | 23/73 |
|---|---|---|---|---|---|---|---|---|---|---|---|---|

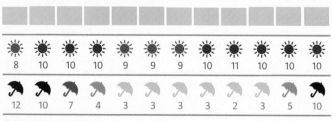

| ☀ | 8 | 10 | 10 | 10 | 9 | 9 | 9 | 10 | 11 | 10 | 10 | 10 |
|---|---|---|---|---|---|---|---|---|---|---|---|---|
| ☂ | 12 | 10 | 7 | 4 | 3 | 3 | 3 | 3 | 2 | 3 | 5 | 10 |
| ≈ | 28/82 | 28/82 | 28/82 | 29/84 | 28/82 | 28/82 | 27/81 | 27/81 | 27/81 | 27/81 | 28/82 | 29/84 |

*(www.peramatour.com)*, which have set timetables, are much less expensive. Residents prefer to take the small local buses *(bemo, colt)* for a few cents – this is a real experience for anybody who is not afraid of close contact and inquisitive questions. Unfortunately, the tourist transport business has almost done away with most of the minibuses in most parts of Bali. You can order a taxi *(Blue Bird Bali: tel. 0361 70 11 11, Blue Bird Lombok: tel. 0370 62 70 00)* in the major centres. The motorbike taxis of *Go-Jek (www.go-jek.com)*, which are ordered by app, are extremely popular (see p. 119). *Uber (www.uber. com/cities/bali/)* and *GrabTaxi (www. grab.com)* are also available in parts of Bali, although legally they are operating in something of a grey area. On Lombok and the Gilis, the *cidomos* and *dokars* (one-horse carriages) are great for travelling short distances. There are fixed prices for *cidomos* on the Gilis.

## TIME

Bali, Lombok and the Gilis are in the Central Indonesian time zone (WITA), which is eight hours ahead of Greenwich Mean Time (GMT) (seven hours during daylight saving time).

## TIPPING

Ten per cent is appropriate in a restaurant if a service charge is not included – in that case, just leave some small change. A chauffeur will be pleased to receive 50,000 Rp after a day trip and – depending on how satisfied you were – you can give a guide 20,000–30,000 Rp.

## WHAT TO WEAR

Skimpy clothing is not appropriate on any of the islands. This also applies to men – especially on official occasions such as appointments with the authorities. Knees and shoulders must always be covered when visiting temples; you can rent a *sarong* at the entrance for a donation or fixed fee if you do not have a suitable wrap-around with you. Light cotton clothing with long sleeves and legs is also the best protection against sunburn and mosquito bites. And, although some female tourists sun themselves topless in Kuta: bathing in the nude is forbidden in Indonesia.

## WHEN TO GO

The best period is the dry season from May to October. It rarely rains continuously in the rainy season from November to April but the heavy tropical downpours often result in flooding in the interior of the country and may limit your activities. The temperature is around 30 °C/86 °F throughout the year but it can be considerably cooler in the mountainous regions. Within the last decade, though, the seasons slipped more and more, so it may well stay dry until December or rain in July.

## WHERE TO STAY

From homestays to luxury hotels – there are all kinds of accommodation options on Bali. Homestays and *losmen* (guesthouses) frequently have no air conditioning and only an Indonesian *mandi* or ladle bath. In the small venues it is often possible to negotiate a discount for longer stays.

Many of the large hotels and villa complexes provide first class service. It is cheaper if you make your internet booking well in advance. Holiday homes with inclusive prices are becoming increasingly popular with families and groups.

# USEFUL PHRASES INDONESIAN

## PRONUNCIATION

To facilitate pronunciation: in general, the penultimate syllable is stressed. The vowels are spoken the same length. Diphthongs **ai**, **au**, **oi** are pronounced as two separate vowels when they appear inside a word, but as one sound when at the end of a word.

| | |
|---|---|
| c | like the **ch** in **ch**eers |
| e | in syllables that are not at the end: unstressed **e** as in st**e**rn |
| | in syllables at the end of a word: stressed **e** as in r**e**d |
| | final syllables: short **a** as in for**ay** |
| ng | eng like the soft **ng** in si**ng**ing |
| ngg | eng like the hard **ng** in bi**ng**o |
| ny | nye like the **ny** in ca**ny**on (similar to the ñ sound in Spanish) |
| kh | kha lie the **ch** in lo**ch** |
| sy | sya like the **sh** in **sh**oe or **sh**ip |

### IN BRIEF

| | |
|---|---|
| Yes/No/Maybe | ya/tidak/mungkin |
| Thank you/Please | Terima kasih!/Tolong! *(asking for help)* |
| | Silakan! *(offer/invitation)* |
| | Sama-sama! *(don't mention it)* |
| Excuse me, please | Maaf! |
| May I ...?/Pardon? | Boleh ...?/Bagaimana? |
| I would like to .../have you got ...? | Saya mau .../Apa ada ...? |
| How much is ...? | Berapa harga ...? |
| I (don't) like this | Saya (tidak) suka. |
| good/bad/broken/doesn't work | baik/jelek/rusak/tidak jalan |
| too much/much/little | terlalu banyak/banyak/sedikit |
| Help!/Attention!/Caution! | Tolong!/Awas!/Hati-hati! |
| ambulance/police/fire brigade | ambulans/polisi/pemadam kebakaran |
| Prohibition/forbidden | larangan/dilarang |
| danger/dangerous | bahaya/berbahaya |
| Can I take a picture of you/here? | Apa saya boleh memotret Anda/di sini? |

### GREETINGS, FAREWELL

| | |
|---|---|
| Good morning!/ afternoon! | Selamat pagi *(until 11am)*/ siang *(11am–3pm)* |

# Kamu berbicara bahasa Indonesia?

"Do you speak Indonesian?" This guide will help you to say the basic words and phrases in Indonesian.

| | |
|---|---|
| Good evening!/night! | sore *(3–6pm)*/malam *(from 6pm)*! |
| Hello!/Goodbye!/See you! | Halo!/Sampai jumpa!/Dada! |
| My name is ... | Nama saya ... |
| What's your name? | Siapa nama Anda?/Siapa nama kamu? |
| I'm from ... | Saya dari ... |

## DATE & TIME

| | |
|---|---|
| Monday/Tuesday | Senen/Selasa |
| Wednesday/Thursday | Rabu/Kamis |
| Friday/Saturday | Jumat/Sabtu |
| Sunday/working day/holiday | Minggu/hari kerja/hari raya |
| today/tomorrow/yesterday | hari ini/besok/kemarin |
| hour/minute | jam/menit |
| day/night/week | hari/malam/minggu |
| month/year | bulan/tahun |
| What time is it? | Jam berapa? |
| It's three o'clock | Jam tiga. |
| It's half past three. | Jam setengah empat. |
| quarter to four | Jam empat kurang seperempat |
| quarter past four | Jam empat lewat seperempat |

## TRAVEL

| | |
|---|---|
| open/closed | buka/tutup |
| departure/arrival | keberangkatan/kedatangan |
| toilets/ladies/gentlemen | kamar kecil/wanita/pria |
| (no) drinking water | (bukan) air minum |
| Where is ...?/Where are ...? | Di mana ...? |
| left/right/straight ahead/back | kiri/kanan/terus/kembali |
| close/far | dekat/jauh |
| bus/minibus/taxi | bis/bemo/taxi |
| (bus) stop/cab stand | haltebis/pangkalan taxi |
| street map/map | peta |
| train station/harbour | stasiun/pelabuhan |
| airport | bandara/airport |
| I would like to rent ... | Saya mau ... sewa. |
| a car/a bicycle | mobil/sepeda |
| a boat | kapal |
| petrol/gas station | pompa bensin |
| petrol (gas)/diesel | bensin/solar |
| breakdown/repair shop | kendaraan rusak/bengkel |

## FOOD & DRINK

| | |
|---|---|
| Could you please book a table for tonight for four? | Tolong reservasi satu meja untuk empat orang nanti malam. |
| The menu, please. | Minta menu. |
| Could I please have ...? | Apa saya tolong bisa mendapat ...? |
| bottle/glass | botol/gelas |
| knife/fork/spoon | pisau/garpu/sendok |
| with/without ice/sparkling | pakai/tanpa es/gas |
| vegetarian/allergy | vegetaris/alergi |
| May I have the bill, please? | Saya mau bayar. |
| bill/receipt/tip | bon/kwitansi/tip, uang rokok |

## SHOPPING

| | |
|---|---|
| Where can I find...? | Di mana ada ...? |
| I'd like .../I'm looking for ... | Saya mau .../Saya cari ... |
| Do you put photos onto CD? | Apa Anda bisa membakar foto di CD? |
| pharmacy/chemist | apotik/toko obat |
| bakery/market | toko roti/pasar |
| shopping centre/department store | pusat pembalanjaan/mall |
| food shop | toko bahan makanan |
| supermarket | supermarket |
| photographic items/newspaper shop | toko foto/kios koran |
| kiosk | warung/kios |
| 100 grammes/1 kilo | seratus gram/satu kilo |
| expensive/cheap/price | mahal/murah/harga |
| more/less | lebih banyak/lebih sedikit |
| organically grown | organik |

## ACCOMMODATION

| | |
|---|---|
| I have booked a room. | Saya sudah reservasi kamar. |
| Do you have any ... left? | Apa masih ada ...? |
| single room | kamar untuk satu orang |
| double room | kamar untuk dua orang |
| breakfast/half board | sarapan/makan pagi dan malam |
| full board | tiga kali makan |
| at the front/seafront | menghadap kedepan/menghadap laut |
| lakefront | menghadap danau |
| shower/sit-down bath/balcony/terrace | shower/mandi/balkon/teras |

## BANKS, MONEY & CREDIT CARDS

| | |
|---|---|
| bank/ATM/pin code | bank/ATM/pin |
| I'd like to change ... | Saya mau menukar ... |

| | |
|---|---|
| cash/credit card | tunai/kartu kredit |
| change | uang kembalian |

## HEALTH

| | |
|---|---|
| doctor/dentist/paediatrician | dokter/dokter gigi/dokter anak-anak |
| hospital/emergency clinic | rumah sakit/bantuan medis darurat |
| fever/pain | demam/rasa sakit |
| diarrhoea/nausea/sunburn | menceret/mual/terbakar matahari |
| inflamed/injured | inflamasi/luka |
| plaster/bandage | plaster/perban |
| ointment/cream | salep/krim |
| pain reliever/tablet/suppository | obat anti-nyeri/tablet/uvula/pil taruh |

## POST, TELECOMMUNICATIONS & MEDIA

| | |
|---|---|
| stamp/letter/postcard | perangko/surat/kartu pos |
| I'm looking for a prepaid card for my mobile. | Saya cari kartu prabayar untuk HP. |
| Do I need a special area code? | Apa saya perlu kode khusus? |
| socket/adapter/charger | stopkontak/adaptor/charger |
| computer/battery/rechargeable battery | komputer/baterai/aki |
| at sign (@) | at |
| internet address (URL)/e-mail address | alamat internet/alamat email |
| internet connection/wi-fi | akses internet/WiFi |
| e-mail/file/print | email/file/cetak |

## LEISURE, SPORTS & BEACH

| | |
|---|---|
| beach | pantai |
| sunshade/lounger | payung/kursi malas |
| low tide/high tide/current | air surut/air pasang/arus |

## NUMBERS

| | | | |
|---|---|---|---|
| 0 | nol/kosong | 11 | sebelas |
| 1 | satu | 12 | dua belas |
| 2 | dua | 80 | delapan puluh |
| 3 | tiga | 90 | sembilan puluh |
| 4 | empat | 100 | seratus |
| 5 | lima | 200 | dua ratus |
| 6 | enam | 1000 | seribu |
| 7 | tujuh | 2000 | dua ribu |
| 8 | delapan | 10000 | sepuluh ribu |
| 9 | sembilan | ½ | setengah |
| 10 | sepuluh | ¼ | seperempat |

# ROAD ATLAS

The green line indicates the Discovery Tour
"Bali, Lombok and the Gili Islands at a glance"
The blue line indicates the other Discovery Tours

All tours are also marked on the pull-out map

Photo: Gunung Agung

# Exploring Bali, Lombok and the Gili Islands

The map on the back cover shows how the area has been sub-divided

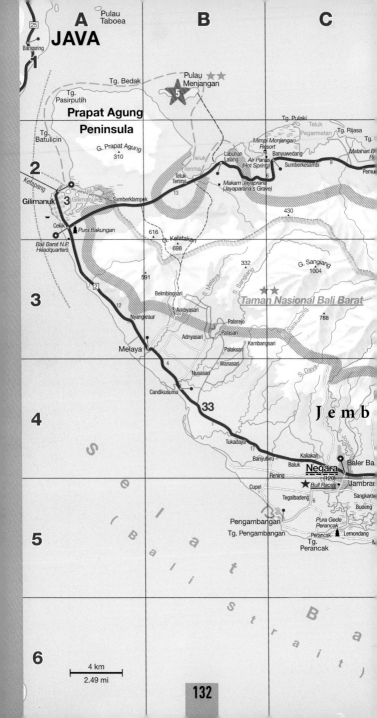

JAVA

A · Pulau Taboea · B · C

25
Bangsring
1

Tg. Bedak
Pulau
Menjangan ★★
5
Prapat Agung
Peninsula
Tg.
Pasirputih

Teluk
Pegarmetan
Tg. Pulaki
Tg. Rijasa
Tg.
Mimpi Menjangan
Resort
Banyuwedang
Matahari B.
Re

Tg.
Batulicin
G. Prapat Agung
310
Teluk
Terima
Labuhan
Lalang
Air Panas
(Hot Spring)
Sumberkesambi
9
Pemu

2
Ketapang
Teluk
Terima
Makam Jayaprana
(Jayaparana's Grave)
6
430

Gilimanuk
3
Gilimanuk
Sumberklampek
13

Cekik
Pura Bakungan

Bali Barat N.P.
Headquarters
616
G. Kelatakan
698
G. Sangiang
1004
332

591
Belimbingsari
Taman Nasional Bali Barat ★★

3
2
12
Nyangkraur
Ambyasari
Palarejo
Palasari
788

Melaya
Adnyasari
Palaksari
Kambangsari

4
Wanasari
Nusasari
Candikusuma
33

Tukadaya
17
Banyubiru
Kaliakah
Jemb

Baluk
Negara
(120)
Baler Ba

Rening
Bull Races
Jambran

Cupel
Tegalbadeng
6
Sangkara

Pengambangan
Tg. Pengambangan
Pura Gede
Perancak
Perancak
Lemondang
Budeng

5
Tg.
Perancak

S e l a t   B a l i

S t r a i t

B a

6
4 km
2.49 mi

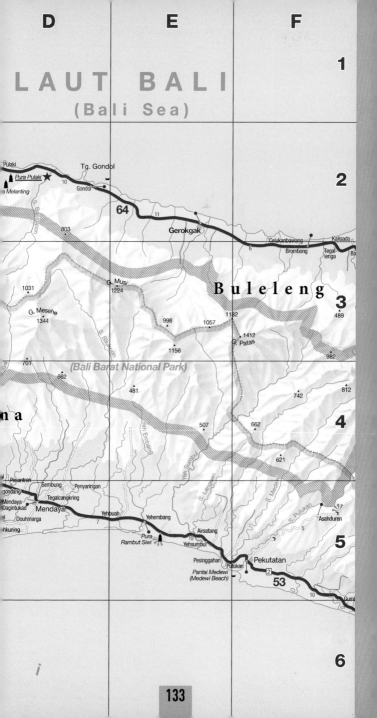

**D**　　　　**E**　　　　**F**

**1**

**2**

**3**

**4**

**5**

**6**

## LAUT BALI
### (Bali Sea)

Pulaki
Pura Pulaki ★
a Melanting
Tg. Gondol
Gondol
10
64
11
803
Gerokgak
Celukanbawang
Brombong
Kalisada
Tegal
lenga
6
Ba

## Buleleng

G. Musi
1224
1031
G. Mesehe
1344
998
1057
1182
489
1156
1412
G. Patas
982
701
*(Bali Barat National Park)*
662
481
742
812
507
662
621
n a
Pesantren
Sembung
Penyaringan
Mendaya
Dagintukad
al
Tegalcangkring
Mendaya
Yehbuah
Yehembang
Airsatang
Asahduren
Douhmarga
hkuning
Pura
Rambut Siwi
Yehsumbul
Pesinggahan
Pulukan
Pekutatan
7
10
5
Pantai Medewi
(Medewi Beach)
53
2
10
Gumi

*i*

133

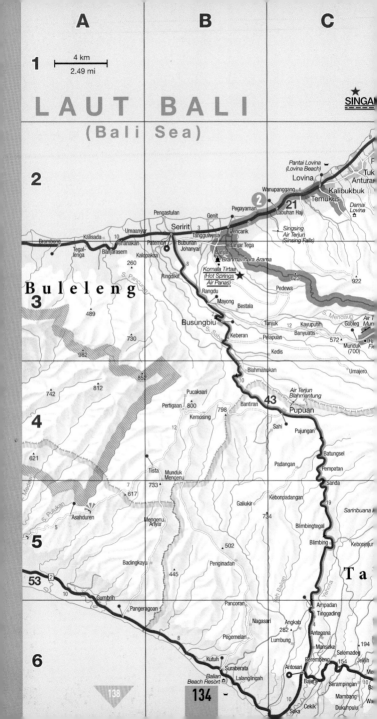

# A    B    C

**1** 4 km / 2.49 mi

## LAUT BALI
### (Bali Sea)

★ SINGA

**2**

Pantai Lovina
(Lovina Beach)
Lovina
Tuk
Antura
Kalibukbuk
Wanupanggang 4
Ternukus
Pegayaman
2    21
Damai
Lovina
Labuhan Haji
Pengastulan
Genit
Seririt    3
Umaanyar    Dencarik    Singsing
Tangguwesia    Air Terjun
Brombong    Kalisada    10    (Sinsing Falls)
Tegal-    Banjarasem    Patemon    Bubunan    Banjar Tega
lenga    Venanakan    Johanyari
Kalopaksa    260    8    Bantang
Ringdikit    Brahmavihara Arama
Komala Tirtaa ★
(Hot Springs
Air Panas)
Rangdu    Pedewa    621    922
**3**    **Buleleng**    Mayong    Bestala
489    Busungbiu    Tunjuk    Kayuputih    Air T
730    Keberan    12    Banyuatis    Gobleg    Mun
Pelapuan    572    R
982    Kedis    Munduk    Fie
(700)
Blahmanakan    Umajero
852    10
742    812    Pucaksari
Pertigaan    800    Bantiran    Air Terjun
798    43    Blahmantung
Kemosing    Pupuan
**4**    12    Sahi
Pujungan
621    Batungsel
Tista    Padangan    Pempatan
Munduk    Sanda
7    Mengenu
733    617    Kebonpadangan    19    Sarinbuana
Galiukir    734
Mengenu    Blimbingtegal
Ariyar    502    Blimbing    Kebonjajur
**5**    Badingkayu    Penginadan    **Ta**
445
Pancoran
53    2    Nagasari    Ampadan
Angkah    Tinggading
10    Gumbrih    Lumbung    Antegana
282
Pangeragoan    Pegemelan    Manseke
8    Berembeng    154    Selemadeg    194
Kutuh    Antosan    Jejih    Be
**6**    Suraberata    Bajera
Balian    Lalanglinggah    Serampingan    Mambang    Wa
Beach Resort    Cekik    Dukuhpulu
138    134    Seka    Me    Bo

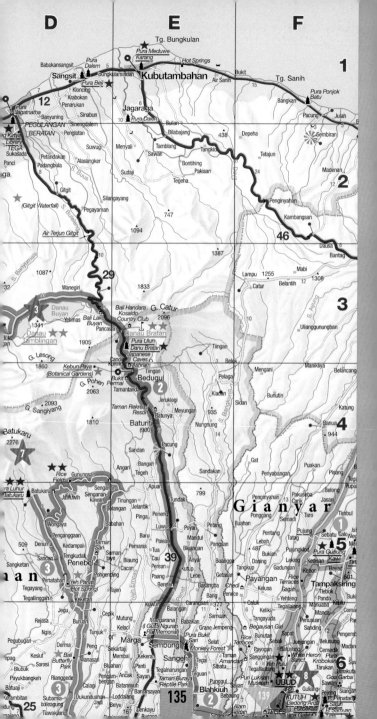

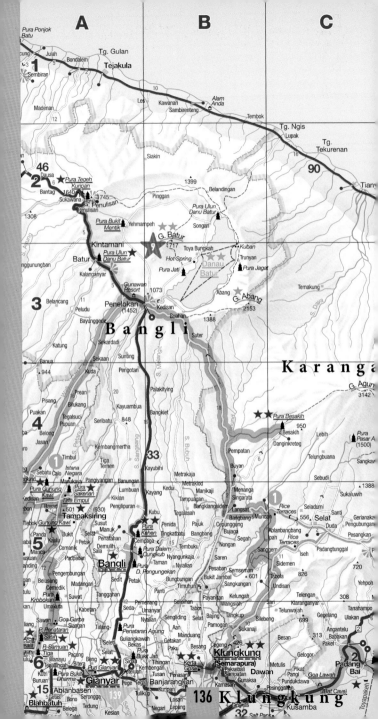

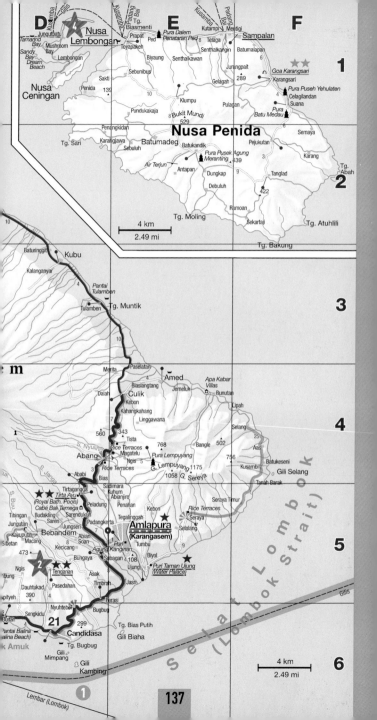

**D**

Jun.gutbatu
Nusa
Lembongan
Mushroom Bay
Lembongan
Tamarind Bay
Sandy Bay
Dream Beach

Nusa
Ceninga

Penangkidan
Karangjawa
Tg. Sari
Sebuluh

**E**

Tg. Biasmenti
Prapat
Ped
Toyapakeh

Biyaung
Senthaikawan

Sebunibus
Sakti
Penida

Pundukakaja

Air Terjun
Antapan

**Nusa Penida**

Batumadeg
Batukandik
Sebuluh

Pura Pusek Agung
Meranting

Dungkap
Debuluh

Rimoan

Sekartaji

Tg. Moling

4 km
2.49 mi

**F**

Kutampi
Mentigi
Telaga
Senthalkangin
**Sampalan**

Batumalapan

Jurangpait
Gelagah    289
Pulagan

Klumpu

Goa Karangsari ★★
Karangsari
Pura Puseh Yehulaten
Celagilandan
Suana
Pura
Batu Medau

Semaya

Pejukutan

Tanglad

Karang

Tg. Abah

422

Tg. Atuhlili

Tg. Bakung

**1**

**2**

Baturinggit
Kalanganyar
Kubu

Pantai
Tulamben
Tulamben   Tg. Muntik

**m**

Merita
Paselatan
Biaslangtang
Dalah   Culik
Kebon
Kahangkahang
Linggawana
Tista
560   343
Rice Terraces
Magatelu
Abang
Ngis
Rice Terraces
Bias
Ababi
Tirtagangga
Tirta Ayu ★★
(Royal Bath. Pools)
Cabé Bali Tamega ★
Peladung
Budakling
Sarendukuh
Saren
Jungseri
Abian
Bebandem   Soan
Macang
Kecicang
Bungaya
Subagan
Asak
473
Ngis
★ ★★
Tengana
Pasedahan
Dauhtukad
390
pityeh
Butan
Sengkidu
**21**
Pantai Balina
(alina Beach)
k Amuk

Amed
Jemeluk
Apa Kabar
Villas
Bunutan

Lipah

Selang

Bangle   502

768
Pura Lempuyang
G. Lempuyang 1175
1058   G. Sereya

Kusambi
Tanah Barak

25

Aas
756

Batukeseni
Gili Selang

Sadimara
Kuhum
Abianjiro
Penahan   Kebon
Tegalinggah
Padangkerta
Puri   Tumbu
Agung Kanginan
108
Ujung   Biyol

Seraya Timur
Rice Terraces
Seraya
Selalang

**Amlapura**
**(Karangasem)** ★

Puri Taman Ujung ★★
(Water Palace)

Jasri

Timbrah
Perasi

Nyuhtebe
Bugbug
299
**Candidasa**
Tg. Bias Putih
Gili Biaha
Tg. Bugbug
Gili
Mimpang   Gili
Kambing

**3**

**4**

**5**

Selat Lombok (Lombok Strait)

Gilis

4 km
2.49 mi

**6**

Lembar (Lombok)   ①

# D

**Gianyar**

Ponggang  Semadi  Timbul  Tiga  **33**  Kayubihi  Pempatan

Buahan  Pentang  Pujung  Calo  Negara  Pangiyangan  Lumbuan  Banunung  Metraklod  **135**  Menanga  Buyan

Lebah  Bukian  Pujungkidul  Sebatu  Pura Gunung  Pura  Pangiyangan  Kedul  Tampuagan  Bangkiangsidem  Singaratta

487  Dasing  Leking  Tatag  Marukaya  Kawi  Sakenan  Kikian  Tegalasah  Bangbang  Langsat  Muncan  Rice

Tangkup  Kedisan  Bayad  Penelokan  Tirta Empul  (630)  Penglipuran  Kubu  Penida  Pajuk  Cepunggung  Sipah  Terraces

Payangan  Gagah  **Tampaksiring**  Susut  Manuk  Bangbang  Bujaga  Segah  Ablanbang

Chedi  Kelusa  Yehteng  Gunung Kawi  Selat  Petak  Penatahan  Nongan  Sanggem  Terr.

Penece  Caluk  Keliki  Rice  Tieblk  Bukit  Demulih  Cempaga  **Pura**  Tembuku  Nyangkunkaja  Saren  Sidem

Tangayuda  Manuaba  Mariga  Terraces  Pande  Comanik  Sala  15  **Kehen**  Pura Dalem  Nyialian  Pesaban  Semeneh  Tabola

Begausan Giri  Padpadan  Cungkub  D. Pengungkan  Bungbungan  Bukit Jambal  601

**Gianyar**  Pengembungan  Sedit  Petak  Sangkungan  Undisan

Rice Terraces  Sebali  Junjungan  Belusang  Madangan  Tanggahan  Panti  Timuhun  Payangan  Kelungah  Sari  Telun

Batuyang  Cemedk  Suwat  Seda  Selisihan  Tabor  Wangsiah

Sanggingan  White Heron  Tarukan  Umakuta  Kroban  Pemenang  Umanyar  Sengliding  Bajing  Tangkup  Silebeng  to

Yeh Pulu  Pura  Senglima  Aan  Manduang  Sukanai  Besar

**UBUD**  Puri Lukisan  Tarukan  Goa Garba  Tojaang  Seleti  Guliangkawah  Bekas  Celakan  Pamogan  **2**

Museum  Guliang  Sayan  Siangan  Pura  Paku  Besang

**PADANGTEGAL**  Gedong Arca  Pejeng  Selat  **Pura**  Kerta

**PELIATAN**  Purtabakala  Basih  Pacung  Pelatean  Petelutan  Kembengan  Penasan  Takmin  Gunaka  Metulis

Goa Gajah  **Pura**  Samuan  Pura Bukit Jati  Tusan  Tangkas  **Dawan**

**PEJENG**  Bedulu  Tiga  Kuri  Sidan  Thingan  Losan  Gelgel  Pun

Monkey  Tegallinggah  Wanayu  Tegal  Pege  **Banjarangkan** Gosa  Kamasan

Forest  Mas  Pura Bona  Buruan  Pelu  **Klungkung**

Kmba  Batusepih  Dharma  Jroagung  Satra  Kamasan

Kelingkung  Kengetan  **Abianbasen**  Bono  **Gianyar**  Tegal  Tulikup  Gelgel  Sidayu  Jumpai  **32**  Kusamba

**Blahbatuh**  Tedung  Serongga  Kesian  Tegallaesan  Trepang  Salt Pans

133  Silakarang  Sibang  Bali Bali  Belega  Medahan  Lebih  Pura Batu Kolok

Silungan  Sakah  Air Terjun  Kebon  Keramas  **Bali Marine &**

Tegal  Mawang  Kemenuh  Tegenungan  Tojan  Pering  **Safari Park**  Pura Segara

Gutri  Belaluwan  Negara  Saba  Pura Masceti

**Singapadu**  Batuan  Rimba Reptile  **Sukawati**  Pinda  Banda  Pura Batu Kiotok

Jagapati  Taman Burung  Centre  Guang  Telabah  Tg. Petanu

Lapiaui  **Celuk**  (95)  **Tebuana**  Rangkan

Bali Bird Park  Negaltamu  Cemeng  Guang  Ketewel

**Batubulan**  Batuaji  Sasih  Pabean

Semaga  Tohpati  44  Akte  Blauan

Kesiman  Gumicik  Padang Galak

**DENPASAR**  **TANJUNGBUNGKAK**  Museum Le Mayeur

Bali  Museum  **Intaran**  **Sanur**

**12**  Sindhu

Sidakarya  Batujimbar

Semawang  Blanjong

Tg. Serangan  Ponjok

Pulau Serangan  (Turtle Island)

njung  enoa

engkilung

Bualu

Nusa Dua  **Nusa Dua**

Pura Geger

ali Resort

# E

# F

Kubu  **1**

**1**

**Klungkung**  **★★**

**Klungkung**  (Semarapura)  Paksebali  **Dawan**

**1**

**K l u n g k u n g**

Kusamba

**★★** **4** Nusa Lembongan  **4**

Tamarind Bay  Jungutbatu  Mushroom  Bay

Sandy Bay  Lembongan  Dream Beach

Nusa  Ceningan

Tg. Sari  **5**

S e l a t   B a d u n g  (B a d u n g   S t r a i t)

Gillis

Lembar (Lombok)  **6**

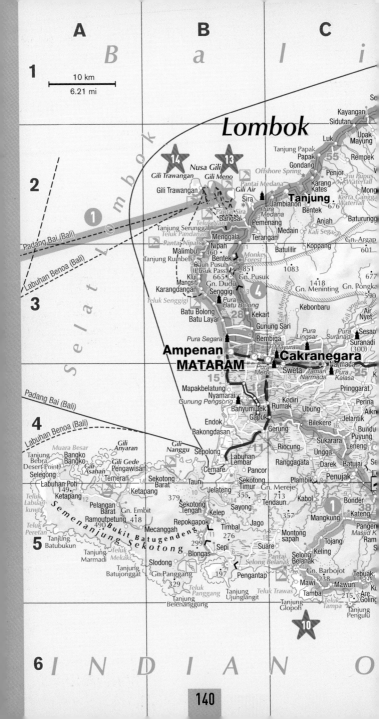

# Lombok

**B a l i**

**10 km**
**6.21 mi**

Kayangan
Sidutan
Luk
Upak
Mayung

Tanjung Papak
Papak
Gondang
⭐ 55
Penjor

Offshore Spring
Karang
Kates

⭐ 14
*Nusa Gili*
⭐ 13

*Gili Trawangan*
*Gili Meno*

Gili Trawangan
*Gili Air*
*Pantai Medana*
Jambianom
676
*Pura Medana*

**Tanjung**

Tu Pupus
*Waterfall*

Mong
Kerta Gangga
*Waterfall*

*Sira*
Bangsal
Pemenang
Bentek

Baturungg

Gn. Argap
601

Padang Bai (Bali)

Tanjung Serunggal
*Teluk Pandanan*
*Pantai Nipah*
Menggala
Terangan
Medain
Anjah
*Kali Segara*

Koppang

**Selat Lombok**

Labuhan Benoa (Bali)

Tanjung Rumbeh
*Nipah*
Bentek
Batulilir

Malimbu
*Monkey Forest*

1083

677
590

Daun Pusuh
(Pusuk Pass) 851
Klui 665
Mangsit
Gn. Dudu
Senggigi
*Gn. Pusuk*

*Batu Bolong*

4

1418
Gn. Meninting Gn. Pongka

Karangdangan

*Teluk Senggigi*

Kebonbaru

Air
Nyet

Batu Bolong
Batu Layar

28
Kekait

Gunung Sari
Rembiga

*Pura Lingsar*
*Pura Suranadi*
Sesao
Suranadi
(300)

*Pura Segara*

P.Mayura

**Ampenan**
**MATARAM**

**Cakranegara**
Narmada
*Pura Kalasa*
25

*Pura Meru*
Sweta
*Taman Narmada*

15

Mapakbelatung
Nyamarai
*Gunung Pengsong*
Banyumulek
Kediri
Rumak
Ubung
Bilekere
Pringgarat
Perina
Aikr

Gapuk
Gerung

Jelantik
Bundu
Puyung
Leneng

Endok
Bakongdasan
Sepolong

Ungga
Sukarara
Darek
Batujai

Cemare
Labuhan
Lembar
Pancor
Riocung
Ranggagata
Plambik
Penujak

Padang Bai (Bali)

Gili
Anyaran
Gili
Nanggu

Gn. Mereje
355
713
Kabol
Bonder
Kateng
38

Labuhan Benoa (Bali)

*Muara Besar*
Bangko
Bangko
Tanjung
Bebra
(Desert Point)
Selegong
*Gili Gede*
Pengawisan
*Gili Asahan*
Temerari
Sekotong
Barat
Taun
Jelateng
Sayong
357
Mangkung
Pangen
Masjid N
Ram

*Teluk Labuhan-kuyet*
Labuhan-Poh
149
Ketapang
Ketapang
Pelangan
Barat
Ramoutpetung
Gn. Embit
418
Sekotong
Tengah
Kelep
Jago
Montong
sapah
Tojang
Keling

*Teluk Peretan*

490

Mecanggah
299
Repokgapok
Timbal
276
Sepi
Suare
Selong
Belanak
Gn. Barbojot
238
Tebuak

Tanjung
Batubukun
Tanjung
Marmadi
Slodong
Gn.Panggang
329
Blongas
197
Pengantap
*Pantai Selong Belanak*
Mawi
Mawun
215
Are-
Goling
Ku

Tanjung
Batujonggat
Tanjung
Mekaki
*Teluk Panggang*
*Teluk Ujunglangit*
*Teluk Trawas*
Tamba
*Teluk Tampa*

Tanjung
Belenanggung
Tanjung
Glopoh
⭐ 10

Tanjung
Tampa
Tanjung
Pengulu

**I N D I A N   O**

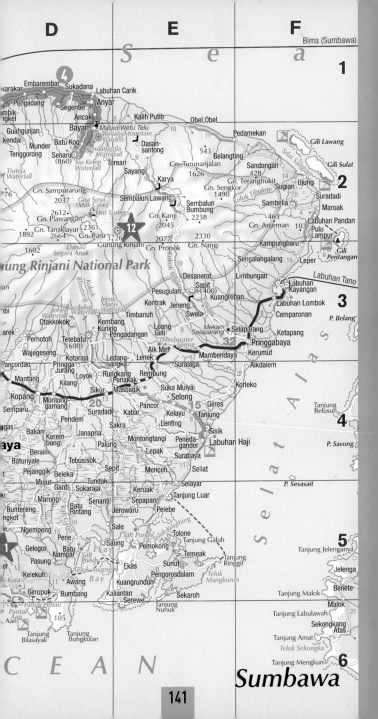

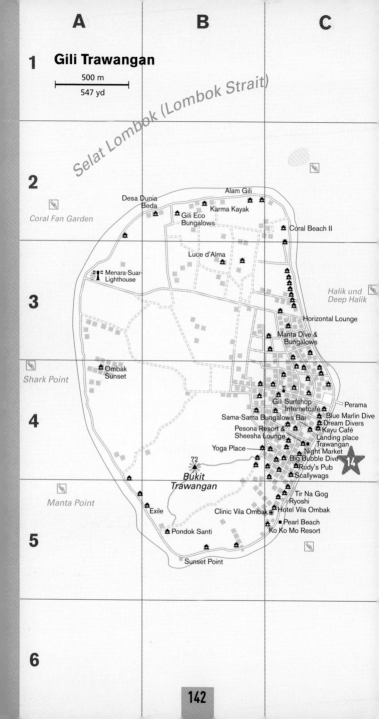

# Gili Trawangan

500 m
547 yd

Selat Lombok (Lombok Strait)

Coral Fan Garden

Desa Dunia Beda

Alam Gili

Karma Kayak

Gili Eco Bungalows

Coral Beach II

Luce d'Alma

Menara-Suar-Lighthouse

Halik und Deep Halik

Horizontal Lounge

Manta Dive & Bungalows

Shark Point

Ombak Sunset

Gili Surfshop

Perama

Internetcafé

Blue Marlin Dive

Sama-Sama Bungalows Bar

Dream Divers

Pesona Resort & Sheesha Lounge

Kayu Café

Landing place

Yoga Place

Trawangan

Night Market

Big Bubble Dive

Rudy's Pub

Scallywags

Bukit Trawangan

72

Manta Point

Tir Na Gog Ryoshi

Exile

Clinic Vila Ombak

Hotel Vila Ombak

Pondok Santi

Pearl Beach

Ko Ko Mo Resort

Sunset Point

142

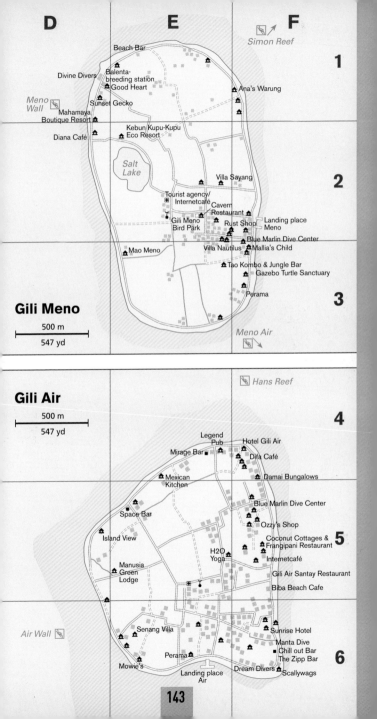

**D**  **E**  **F**

**1**

Beach Bar
Divine Divers
Balenta-breeding station
Good Heart
Sunset Gecko
Ana's Warung

Meno Wall
Mahamaya Boutique Resort
Diana Café
Kebun Kupu-Kupu Eco Resort

**2**

Salt Lake

Villa Sayang
Tourist agency/Internetcafé
Cavern Restaurant
Gili Meno Bird Park
Rust Shop
Landing place Meno
Blue Marlin Dive Center
Mao Meno
Villa Nautilus
Mallia's Child
Tao Kombo & Jungle Bar
Gazebo Turtle Sanctuary
Perama

**Gili Meno**

500 m
547 yd

**3**

Meno Air

---

Hans Reef

**Gili Air**

500 m
547 yd

**4**

Legend Pub
Hotel Gili Air
Mirage Bar
Difa Café
Damai Bungalows
Mexican Kitchen
Blue Marlin Dive Center
Space Bar
Ozzy's Shop
Island View
Coconut Cottages & Frangipani Restaurant
H2O Yoga
Internetcafé
Manusia Green Lodge
Gili Air Santay Restaurant
Biba Beach Cafe

**5**

Air Wall
Senang Villa
Sunrise Hotel
Manta Dive
Chill out Bar
The Zipp Bar
Perama
Mowie's
Dream Divers
Scallywags
Landing place Air

**6**

# KEY TO ROAD ATLAS

Straße mit zwei getrennten Fahrbahnen
Dual carriage-way

Durchgangsstraße
Thoroughfare

Wichtige Hauptstraße
Important main road

Hauptstraße
Main road

Sonstige Straße
Other road

Fahrweg, Piste
Carriage way, track

Karrenweg, Fußweg
Mule-track, footpath

Straßen in Bau
Roads under construction

⚲ 49 ⚲ Großkilometer
Long distances in km

⚲ 10 ⚲ Kleinkilometer
Short distances in km

Fernverkehrsbahn
Main line railway

Autofähre
Car ferry

Schifffahrtslinie
Shipping route

Sumpf
Swamp

Mangrove
Mangrove

Korallenriff
Coral reef

Landschaftlich besonders schöne Strecke
Route with beautiful scenery

◄ 15% Bedeutende Steigungen
Important gradients

**DENPASAR** Verwaltungssitz
Administrative capital

Verkehrsflughafen
Airport

Flugplatz
Airfield

★★ **UBUD**

★ **Krambitan**

★★ *Danau Bratan*

★ *Kebun Paya*

**Kultur**
**Culture**

Eine Reise wert
Worth a journey

Lohnt einen Umweg
Worth a detour

**Landschaft**
**Landscape**

Eine Reise wert
Worth a journey

Lohnt einen Umweg
Worth a detour

Besonders schöner Ausblick
Important panoramic view

Nationalpark, Naturpark
National park, nature park

4807 Bergspitze mit Höhenangabe in Metern
Mountain summit with height in metres

(630) Ortshöhe
Elevation

Kloster, Tempel, Heiligtum (buddhistisch)
Monastery, temple, shrine (Buddhist)

Tempel, Heiligtum (hinduistisch)
Temple, shrine

Schloss, Burg
Palace, castle

Denkmal
Monument

Wasserfall
Waterfall

Höhle
Cave

Ruinenstätte
Ruins

Sonstiges Objekt
Other object

Golfplatz
Golf-course

Jugendherberge
Youth hostel

Badestrand
Bathing beach

Tauchen
Diving

MARCO POLO Highlight

MARCO POLO Erlebnistour 1
MARCO POLO Discovery Tour 1

MARCO POLO Erlebnistouren
MARCO POLO Discovery Tours

# FOR YOUR NEXT TRIP...

# MARCO POLO TRAVEL GUIDES

The travel guides with
**Insider Tips**

# INDEX

This index lists all places, sights and destinations featured in this guide. Numbers in bold indicate a main entry.

CREDITS

# WRITE TO US

e-mail: info@marcopologuides.co.uk

Did you have a great holiday? Is there something on your mind? Whatever it is, let us know! Whether you want to praise, alert us to errors or give us a personal tip – MARCO POLO would be pleased to hear from you.

We do everything we can to provide the very latest information for your trip.

Nevertheless, despite all of our authors' thorough research, errors can creep in. MARCO POLO does not accept any liability for this. Please contact us by e-mail or post.

MARCO POLO Travel Publishing Ltd
Pinewood, Chineham Business Park
Crockford Lane, Chineham
Basingstoke, Hampshire RG24 8AL
United Kingdom

**PICTURE CREDITS**
Cover photograph: Banjar Tegehe, Bali (Laif: F. Heuer)
Photos: huber-images: M. Brook (5, 43), A. Pavan (67), R. Schmid (59), K. Trubavin (39, 60, 68, 69, 74/75, 76, 122); © iStockphoto/webphotographeer (18 top); Laif: F. Heuer (1 top, 20/21); Laif/hemis: F. Guiziou (114/115), C. Moirenc (44); Laif.hemis.fr (9, 82); Laif/Hemispheres (12/13); Laif/Polaris: P. Oliosi (25); mauritius images: Kugler (117), A. Ridder (64); mauritius images/age: R. Dirschel (34); mauritius images/Alamy (front flap left, front flap right, 32/33, 56, 92, 130/131), T. Cockrem (17), C. Deeney (95), J. Fritz (71), C. Hopkins (81), E. Hulme (36), Ivoha (78), G. Sioen (18 centre), F. Stark (115), S. Thomas (7); mauritius images/Alamy (3); mauritius images/Alamy/Captured Soul (107); mauritius images/Alamy/dbimages (113, 114); mauritius images/Alamy/Design Pics Inc (19 below); mauritius images/Alamy/FLPA (116/117); mauritius images/Alamy/Robertharding (86); mauritius images/Alamy/travelstock44 (63); mauritius images/Alamy/Zoonar GmbH (4 top); mauritius images/Blend Images: C. Anderson (19 top); mauritius images/Cultura/Steve Woods Photography (110/111); mauritius images/Hemis.fr: F. Guiziou (90/91); mauritius images/ib: J. W. Alker (11); mauritius images/Image Source (18 below); mauritius images/Imagebroker: M. Moxter (89), K. Petersen (103); mauritius images/Loop Images: E. Nathan (118 top); mauritius images/Photononstop: J. Garcia (85); mauritius images/Westend61: K. Trubavin (2, 52); Schapowalow /4Corners: K. Trubavin (4 below); Schapowalow /SIME: A. Pavan (118 below); Schapowalow: G. Cozzi (49), O. Stadler (119); Schapowalow/4Corners: B. Mitchell (22, 98/99), K. Trubavin (97); Schapowalow/SIME: T. & B. Morandi (6), L. Vaccarella (14/15), O. Stadler (8, 10, 26/27, 28 left, 28 right, 29, 30, 30/31, 41); T. Stankiewicz (55); M. Thomas (46, 50, 72, 116); White Star: Reichelt (31)

**2nd edition 2018 – fully revised and updated**
Worldwide Distribution: Marco Polo Travel Publishing Ltd, Pinewood, Chineham Business Park, Crockford Lane, Basingstoke, Hampshire RG24 8AL, United Kingdom. Email: sales@marcopolouk.com
© MAIRDUMONT GmbH & Co. KG, Ostfildern
Chief editor: Marion Zorn
Author: Christina Schott; editor: Ulrike Frühwald
Programme supervision: Stephan Dürr, Lucas Forst-Gill, Susanne Heimburger, Nikolai Michaelis, Martin Silbermann, Kristin Wittemann; picture editor: Gabriele Forst; What's hot: wunder media, München, Christina Schott
Cartography road atlas: © MAIRDUMONT, Ostfildern; cartography pull-out map: © MAIRDUMONT, Ostfildern
Cover design, p. 1, pull-out map cover: Karl Anders – Büro für Visual Stories, Hamburg; design inside: milchhof:atelier, Berlin; design Discovery Tours, p. 2/3: Susan Chaaban Dipl.-Des. (FH)
Translated from German by Robert Scott McInnes and Mo Croasdale
Editorial office: SAW Communications, Redaktionsbüro Dr. Sabine A. Werner, Mainz: Julia Gilcher, Kristin Smolinna, Cosima Talhouni, Dr. Sabine A. Werner
Prepress: SAW Communications, Mainz, in cooperation with alles mit Medien, Mainz
Phrase book in cooperation with Ernst Klett Sprachen GmbH, Stuttgart, Editorial by Pons Wörterbücher

MIX
Paper from
responsible sources
FSC® C124385

# DOS & DON'TS 👆

A few things to bear in mind while on holiday in Bali

## DO AVOID CHEAP ALCOHOL

Be wary of very cheap cocktails and spirits: they are often mixed with home-brewed palm or rice liquor that is manufactured unprofessionally or adulterated with poisonous additives. In recent years there have been cases of methanol poison – something that can even lead to death.

## DON'T BUY ANY DRUGS

Hashish, ecstasy and magic mushrooms are offered for sale on every street corner in the tourist centres. On no account should you enter into any such deals! There are severe penalties for drug possession and in particularly serious cases conviction can even lead to a death sentence. No exceptions are made for foreigners.

## DON'T PUT YOUR FEET UP

Feet are considered impure and should not be put up in public. You should not climb around on walls or statues in temples for the same reason.

## DO BE SENSITIVE ABOUT CORAL REEFS

Avoid walking on coral reefs, doing so not only damages the highly sensitive ecosystem but is also dangerous. Corals can be very sharp and there are also poisonous coral creatures that should not be touched.

## DO TREAT SACRED SPRINGS WITH RESPECT

Anybody who desecrates a sacred spring by bathing in it will not only attract the wrath of the gods but also have to cover the costs of the spiritual purification that is necessary afterwards.

## DON'T EAT TURTLES

Although officially only allowed on special occasions, some dealers offer turtle eggs, meat and shell for sale. These animals are under threat of extinction so you should definitely decline any offers! The same applies to shark fins, which are cut off of the animals while they are still alive.

## DON'T DISTURB TEMPLE CEREMONIES

Tourists are welcome to attend most ceremonies as long as they know how to behave themselves properly: wear a *sarong* with a sash, don't walk around in front of those praying, never sit higher than the priest and never point a camera directly in somebody's face.

## DO BE PATIENT

If you become impatient waiting or bargaining you will achieve nothing at all! As a rule, you will get much further with a friendly smile. You should avoid any forms of bribery.